ELECTRIC STEEL

AND OTHER ESSAYS

Studies in Comparative Literature
Jadavpur University

Studies in Comparative Literature, Jadavpur University is founded on the view that the study of literatures and the arts in multilingual and culturally diverse contexts such as India demands a comparative approach. It is informed by an interdisciplinary and intercultural focus on *bhasha* literatures, translation, orality and performance as well as other arts and digital humanities, in the context of local, national and international literary and cultural transactions. The series is meant for students, scholars and teachers of comparative literature as well as of single literature and other humanities departments. It brings together the work of faculty members and scholars at the Department of Comparative Literature, Jadavpur University, as well as of national and international visiting scholars who have enriched its research and debates.

Sub-series I: Texts, Contexts, Methods

Ia. Histories and Paradigms
Ib. Approaching New Challenges, Recasting Paradigms

Sub-series II: Indian and Asian Contexts

Sub-series III: Literature and Other Knowledge Systems

IIIa. Literary Studies and Performance
IIIb. Literature and Indigenous Knowledge Systems

Sub-series IV: Lecture Series

Contributions based on talks by Visiting Scholars

STUDIES IN COMPARATIVE LITERATURE
JADAVPUR UNIVERSITY

SUB-SERIES IV: LECTURES

ELECTRIC STEEL

Parallel Stories from Italy, India and the Americas

AND OTHER ESSAYS

Alessandro Portelli

Orient BlackSwan

ELECTRIC STEEL AND OTHER ESSAYS

ORIENT BLACKSWAN PRIVATE LIMITED

Registered Office
3-6-752 Himayatnagar, Hyderabad 500 029, Telangana, India
E-mail: centraloffice@orientblackswan.com

Other Offices
Bengaluru, Chennai, Guwahati, Hyderabad, Kolkata,
Mumbai, New Delhi, Noida, Patna, Visakhapatnam

First published 2023

ISBN 978-93-5442-359-8

Typeset in Adobe Garamond Pro 12.5/15.6 *by*
Shine Graphics, Delhi 110 094

036802

Printed at
Thompson Press, New Delhi 110020

Published by
Orient Blackswan Private Limited
3-6-752, Himayatnagar, Hyderabad 500 029, Telangana, India
E-mail: info@orientblackswan.com

Contents

Publisher's Acknowledgments

"What Makes Oral History Different" from *The Death of Luigi Trastulli and Other Stories: Form and Meaning in Oral History*, pp. 45–58. Copyright © 1991 State University of New York, published by State University of New York Press. Reproduced with permission.

"A Dialogical Relationship: An Approach to Oral History" was previously published as "A Relationship Work: Observations on Oral History", *Salesian Historical Research*, XIX, 1 (36), January–June 2000, 125–34. Reproduced with permission.

General Introduction

The first full-fledged department of Comparative Literature in India, and the second in Asia, was established in Calcutta at Jadavpur University in 1956. The reputed Bangla poet, writer and scholar Buddhadeva Bose was its founder and the first Head of the Department. The *Jadavpur Journal of Comparative Literature*, launched here in 1961, is one of the oldest journals in Asia that has continued, regularly, to publish significant research in comparative literature by national and international scholars. In the late 1980s the UGC earmarked the department for promotion of teaching and research under its Special Assistance Programme. In the early nineties the department widened its areas of interest to first introduce courses in the literatures and cultures of Bangladesh, Africa, Canada and Latin America; then it set up centres in the latter three, subsequently a Centre for Translation of Indian Literatures, and, most recently, a Centre for Studies of Islamicate Asia. During the Tenth Plan the department was also selected by the UGC to participate in its ASIHSS (Assistance for Strengthening of Infrastructure for Humanities and Social Sciences) programme. In addition to these UGC programmes and these centres, the UPE—University with Potential for Excellence—programme of the UGC also enabled the establishment of research projects in the department. These included translation and intercultural studies under Project Anuvad; documentation and research relating to performers of traditional dramatic forms in different districts of West Bengal under Project Palagaan; and a unique new venture involving an exploration of Kolkata through narratives of sound under the project Soundscapes. The first and so far only UGC Centre of Advanced Study in Comparative Literature in India was also established in this department in 2005, and it continued promoting research into its third phase. This series, Studies in Comparative Literature, Jadavpur University, is rooted in this academic history of over six decades.

When other departments of Comparative Literature finally began to be established in India in the 1990s, a sharing of our research and pedagogic experience became imperative. As the practice of comparative literature proliferated in centres and newly established departments as well as in single literature departments right across India, we began to face persistent requests for enhanced access to our research from academics, researchers and students alike. Our research, while considerable, had largely been published by local presses and the university, and did not have the national outreach now demanded of it. It was in response to this need that the idea of initiating a series with a reputed mainstream national publisher came about, and we are especially happy about this partnership with Orient BlackSwan, given the important role it has played in the dissemination of scholarship on Indian literatures and cultures.

We hold that the study of literatures and the arts in multilingual and culturally diverse countries such as ours demands a comparative approach; hence, Studies in Comparative Literature, Jadavpur University, is a series for students, scholars and teachers of comparative literature as well as of single literature, arts and other humanities departments. It explores a range of histories, theoretical reflections, as well as innovative approaches and concerns relevant to the field of comparative literature. In keeping with the basic imperatives of comparative literature, it is both intercultural and interdisciplinary in that it engages with the trajectories of literatures across cultures as well as with the relations between literatures and other fields of creative expression. It is thus informed by an interdisciplinary and intercultural focus on *bhasha* literatures, translation, orality and performance as well as other arts and digital humanities, in the context of local, national and international literary and cultural transactions, and also those of the borderlands.

This series brings together the work of faculty and scholars at the department of Comparative Literature, Jadavpur University, and of national and international visiting scholars. It comprises both edited volumes and authored books, as well as monographs by visiting scholars. The series launches the research carried out under the third phase of the UGC Centre of Advanced Study in Comparative Literature, and the publication of these volumes, we hope, will mark the beginnings of a renewed mapping of comparative literary studies in India.

The current studies build on the foundations of creative intellectual vision, innovative pedagogy and several decades of original scholarship that went into the shaping of what was a new field of study, in fact a new mode of inquiry, in the Indian university. Many generations have enriched comparative literary studies in India, and it is impossible to chart all the contributions of even just those at the Department of Comparative Literature at Jadavpur University in the space of a short introduction such as this. What follows however is a brief account of the directions of research, and of the kinds of publications that emerged from this research, as well as in response to pedagogic needs at this department; it is being presented here as an academic contextualisation for the present series that may be useful to other scholars, centres and departments of not just comparative literature but also literary studies in general.

Before mapping the broad areas of research across the decades however, it may be relevant to reflect for a moment on the intellectual and creative range of teachers and scholars who contributed to its making. Buddhadeva Bose and Sudhindranath Dutta were towering modern Bangla poets and writers, and amongst the foremost intellectuals of their time. Joining them in the early years were Fr. Robert Antoine, a Belgian Jesuit priest who was a Sanskritist and a scholar of Greek and Latin, who translated Kalidasa's *Raghuvamsa* from the Sanskrit into English, and also collaborated on a translation of Virgil's *Aeneid* from the Latin into Bangla; Fr. Pierre Fallon, who was also a Belgian Jesuit priest, a professor of French literature, a licenciate in philosophy and theology and an expert in Bangla philology; and David J. McCutchion who had trained in French and German at Jesus College Cambridge, and later became an authority on both the terracotta temples as well as the *patuas* (scroll painters) of Bengal. The next two generations of teacher-scholars, five of whom also trained in M.A. or Ph.D. programmes of North American departments of Comparative Literature and others in France or Germany, included Naresh Guha, Amiya Dev, Deepak Mazumdar, Subir Roychowdhury, Swapan Mazumdar, Bijoya Das, Subha Chakraborty Dasgupta, Ipsita Chanda, Suman Ghosh, Alokeranjan Dasgupta, Pranabendu Dasgupta, Manabendra Bandyopadhyay, Nabaneeta Dev Sen, Sibaji Bandyopadhyayand Debiprasad Bhattacharya. All of them earned international repute as scholars, and while the last was a polyglot and a renowned Sanskritist, the penultimate five were also major creative writers in Bangla.

It is perhaps the wide range of exposure and training, which was as rigorous as it may seem eclectic, that cautioned scholars of this department about strait-jacketing comparative literary studies into any definitive 'school' or methodology, or of limiting Indian literary studies within the political borders of the Indian nation state. So, even in their pioneering role, they refrained from formulating a Jadavpur 'school' of Comparative Literature, or privileging any comparative methodology over others. They also desisted from confining literary studies to inter-Indian literary relations only, and conscientiously trained their lenses on the wider South-Asian and Asian, Perso-Arabic and Anglo-European fields too; and eventually they reached out to Latin America, Africa and Australia, especially in relation to transactions with Indian literatures and cultures, but also otherwise. Such catholicity, in both approach and range, would naturally give rise to questions of delimitation and focus—and what emerges clearly as a connecting thread across the decades is that, in terms of both literary-cultural focus and methodological approach, scholars here responded to the ground realities and the needs of their times.

It was in the early 1990s that the consolidated programme of publishing started, supported by the Special Assistance Programme of the UGC; the focus in this decade was clearly on creating resources for research. Bibliographies of reception—of World Literature in Bangla periodicals, and of Bangla literature in South Indian languages—formed one thrust area. Translation became a focal point from the beginning: translation of material such as literary manifestoes in Indian languages, and discussions regarding the aesthetics as well as comparative literature methodologies of translation featured in this phase. Literary historiography in India featured as an important concern as did East–West literary interactions of the colonial period. The fourth area of concern was in relation to third-world contexts—to cultures of silence as well as the challenge of envisioning their futures—and this included reflection on African and Latin American literatures and cultures.

The focus on generating resources for comparative research continued through the next five years with translations across several genres (poetry, short stories, plays and excerpts of autobiographies) and several languages (that is, from Bangla into other languages such as Asamiya and English, and from Odia, Gujarati, Marathi and other Indian languages into English as well as Bangla). Also, the first phase had documented debates on comparative literary approaches to historiography; this one brought into focus issues of genology from a comparative perspective, with a volume tracing the *charit* as a genre. A third area of engagement was that of linguistic and cultural formations of self-identity across the literatures of Bengal and Bangladesh, thus bringing the literature of Bangladesh into the purview of our research. This phase was also marked by the publication of three volumes under the rubric of Literary Studies in India: on Literary Historiography, Thematology and Genology; it brought together reflections of comparative literature academics as well as scholars from other literature and humanities departments, on approaches to literary studies in India at the beginning of the twenty-first century.

In the first phase of the Centre of Advanced Study (2005–2010), we continued, on the one hand with the task of generating resources for research, such as the annotated bibliography of Bangla and Asamiya histories of literature;

on the other hand we extended the work on historiography to specific areas of study such as Indian English literature. Two new sets of concerns came into focus in this period. One set related to the need to document and study the fast-disappearing body of folk performances—the outcomes included the recordings and studies of *Manasamangal pala* and *Banabibir pala.* The other set of concerns was underlined by the realisation that most of our international focus had been on literary relations with the Anglo-European world, while those with other Asian cultures had not received the attention they deserved; thus the imperative to retrieve and explore these resulted in a focus on travel literature from Asia with focus on the collection of literary material along sea and trade routes, and the publication of a bibliography of travelogues to Asian countries in Bangla as well as an anthology of Bangla and Odia writings on colonial Burma. During this phase the additional support from the Assistance for Strengthening of Infrastructure for Humanities and Social Sciences (ASIHSS) programme of the UGC enabled research in South Asian contexts and resulted in the publication of a South Asian nationalisms reader, as well as a volume on the poetics and politics of Sufism and Bhakti in South Asia.

The following years, in the second phase of the CAS, were marked by more extensive and deeperresearch in the fields already marked out. At least three areas that had clearly emerged as thrust areas were:

- Comparative Literature: Explorations in Discipline and Methodology
- Roots and Routes: Intra-Indian and Intra-Asian Linguistic, Literary and Cultural Relations
- Literature and Other Knowledge Systems

Resources generated for research during this period included a handbook on terms and concepts in comparative literature, a volume on comparative literature in Germany, and textbooks on Indian Nepali literature in English and Bangla. The publications on comparative explorations in genre included a study of the *namah*. Research on folk cultures as knowledge systems resulted in publications on *charak* and *gajan* in Bengal, another on Karbi oral traditions in the Northeast, as well as a volume on literatures and oratures as knowledge systems, based on texts from Northeast India. A comparative study on the *ghumantoo* roadies, or wanderers, of India and Canada added to this set. In the context of Asian studies, research was published on tales of medieval China. The research on South Asia extended itself to comparative studies of the literatures and cultures of borders in South Asia and the Americas; this last volume marked entry into a new area of research—Comparative Border Studies.

The present series has been envisioned as follows:

Studies in Comparative Literature, Jadavpur University

Sub-series I: Texts, Contexts, Methods

1a. Histories and Paradigms
1b. Approaching New Challenges, Recasting Paradigms

Sub-series II: Indian and Asian Contexts

Sub-series III: Literature and Other Knowledge Systems

IIIa. Literary Studies and Performance
IIIb. Literature and Indigenous Knowledge Systems

Sub-series IV: Lecture Series

Contributions based on talks by Visiting Scholars

In many ways it marks a deepening and consolidation of perspectives across the earlier decades of research; in other ways it also charts new directions in comparative literary studies. The sub-series **Texts, Contexts, Methods** includes two histories in the section *Histories and Paradigms*—one of the emergence and establishment of Indian Comparative Literature, the other a disciplinary and institutional history of comparative literature in India, based on documents preserved at Jadavpur as well as gathered from across the country. Planned along with these are anthologies on texts, contexts and concepts, and on comparative literary studies in India, with contributions from scholars across the country. The section *Approaching New Challenges, Recasting Paradigms* will introduce research in new directions that responds to contemporary challenges. Comparative Literature as a discipline has historically crossed borders in terms of time and space. One of these volumes is a response to the now pervasive trans-national histories of migrants and refugees and, focussing on the Indo-Bangladesh border, it marks a shift from the prism of the 'national' to the prism of borders and frontiers, to the epistemological perspectives of 'borderlanders'; another volume charts the transformations in comparative literary studies in light of the mutual interactions between digital humanities and literary mapping in South Asia.

The sub-series **Indian and Asian Contexts** includes both intra-Indian literary translations and a mapping of linguistic, literary and cultural relations grouped under the rubric of *Roots and Routes*, as well as translations from Bangla and Urdu of fictional and discursive writings of Muslim literati in Bengal from the early twentieth century onward. Included in this sub-series are comparative studies of 'progressive' literatures, South Asian studies of transnational writers such as Ismat Chughtai, and studies of intra-Asian engagements such as Bengal's encounters with Japan in the twentieth century.

The third sub-series, **Literature and Other Knowledge Systems**, includes a volume on reflections on methodology in the translation of performance texts in the sub-section *Literary Studies and Performance*; the sub-section on *Literature and Indigenous Knowledge Systems* carries a comparative study of Karbi and Chakma narrative traditions of Northeast India, as well as another of creation songs from India, Canada, Australia and Southeast Asia.

Finally, the **Lecture Series** comprises volumes based on talks delivered by national and international visiting scholars who have enriched the research and debates of our department, and often taken us in new directions too. We are truly grateful to Alessandro Portelli, Professor Emeritus, University of Rome La Sapienza, and Tridip Suhrud, Professor and Provost, CEPT University, Ahmedabad, for their contributions on oral history and Gandhi's languages respectively, and for their generosity in permitting us to include earlier landmark essays in their volumes. We also extend our gratitude to Robert P Goldman, Professor, University of California at Berkeley, and Daniel Rycroft, Associate Professor at the University of East Anglia for having agreed to write for us on the Valmiki *Ramayana* and the humanities in India, respectively. We thank other scholars, who have collaborated in the research on some of our publications; they include Jatin Nayak, former Professor of Utkal University, Indranil Acharya, Professor at Vidyasagar University, Subha Chakraborty Dasgupta former Professor in our own department, Shraddhanjali Tamang, also a faculty member at Jadavpur University, and writer Manoranjan Byapari.

This series is the collaborative effort of all the faculty members of the Comparative Literature department: Suchorita Chattopadhyay, Kunal Chattopadhyay, Aveek Majumder, Sayantan Dasgupta, Sujit Kumar Mandal, Parthasarathi Bhaumik, Epsita Halder, Debashree Dattaray and Sumit Kumar Barua. They have been working concertedly towards its publication over the last several years; and while the individual volumes will carry their respective names as authors, editors and co-authors, it needs to be put on record that this series is finally seeing the light of day through one of the most devastating pandemics in history only because of their determined collective commitment and mutual intellectual inspiration. We are also grateful to our research fellows—who will be acknowledged individually in the respective volumes—for their selfless and cheerful support. Last but not least we extend our deep gratitude to Padmaja Anant of Orient BlackSwan for her wisdom and infinite patience—it has indeed been a pleasure working with her.

Kavita Panjabi
Samantak Das
Sucheta Bhattacharya
Series Editors

The first volumes of this series are being sent to the press with a heavy heart, for Samantak Das is with us no more. May the infallible spirit with which he contributed to the making of this series continue to enrich it in the years to come.

Electric Steel: Parallel Stories from Italy, India and the Americas

Introduction

The Terni–Igatpuri connection is a good example of the serendipity that many times accompanies the work of oral history. A lifetime of commitment to the heart of the town where I grew up (Terni) on one side; a chance encounter and a brief return (Igatpuri) on the other. And another connection, too: the reason I was driving by the ThyssenKrupp plant in Igatpuri was that I had been invited to meet with Abhivyakti, a rural media for development cooperative in Nashik, because I had met their organisers at a residential seminar in Bellagio (Italy) organised by the Center for Rural Strategies in Whitesburg, Kentucky, United States—another long-term commitment, Appalachian working-class history, on the other side of the ocean, leading to a brief but significant collaboration in India. Ironically, it was two rural cooperatives devoted to agricultural development that led to an industrial project about two steel factories (meanwhile, I had also consulted and used a set of interviews with the workers of another ThyssenKrupp plant in Belo Horizonte made by the Museo da Pessoa in São Paulo). It all goes to show the complexity of relationships in the globalised world in which we live: Italy, India, the United States, Brazil—literally, four continents.

As always, however, the connections are undergirded by difference. A basic difference in these experiences was the relationship between the industrial environment and the rural background. The factory in Terni had been dropped upon a rural and semi-rural area and culture, but in the space of almost a century and a half it had become the heart of the economy and the culture; Terni workers had a family memory of rural origins but were proud industrial workers to the bone. In Igatpuri, on the other hand, not only was the factory a more recent development, employing first-generation workers who felt a degree of nostalgia for the land, the village, and its way of life; but, more importantly, the steel plant was surrounded by a still thriving rural culture that was seeking ways to survive and grow on its own terms.

In the evening of the first day of my first visit, Nitin Paranjape, the founder of Abhyviakti, took us to the rural village of Dhondhegoan. The visit was unplanned, which made the spontaneous welcome—especially by the women and the children—all the more moving and exciting. For hours, we sat on rugs in a circle in which men (including myself) were much on the margin, while the ladies exchanged stories and thoughts about farming and rural culture with my wife Mariella Eboli (a rural economist and sociologist), and the children came and went, listening and giggling. We heard about the effort to make the land produce enough to support the people, through hard work, savings, minicredit, and the intelligent use of shared local knowledge. A lady (who had used minicredit to buy goats and a piece of land and lift herself and family from deep poverty) told us how she and her family had been taught by their elders to use natural fertilizers; when they noticed that their neighbours' fields, raised on chemicals, looked much better, she said, 'we discussed it among ourselves, and realized that while they looked better, in the end their crops were less than ours. So we stuck to the traditional ways.' In the conversation, we agreed that the story was exemplary because the old way was not chosen out of passive submission to the authority of tradition or of the elders, or because 'we always did it that way.' Rather, tradition was tested rationally on the basis of experience, and found to be the better way still. The key phrase was 'we discussed it': the essence of an intelligent, critical use of cultural memory.

Some of the ladies pointed out that families no longer take as many pains as in the past to teach the children what they know. Yet, watching the dozen or so children of all ages sitting around the circle and listening intently, I could not help but remark that knowledge is often passed among the generations not by formal instruction but is absorbed simply because the children are around to hear adults talk and watch them work. The point was taken.

The other difference concerns the power dynamics in the interview. On the same day, in Nashik, I also had an opportunity to talk about oral history to the faculty and students of the local Architectural College, one of the best in the country. Once again, for most of those in attendance this was the first exposure to the concept of oral history, and they were deeply interested, especially in the connection between the historical memory inherent in spaces and buildings and the work of architects and planners. There was a lively question-and-answer session; my favorite question was: 'Since you are from Italy, can you tell us about Antonio Gramsci?' I was glad to comply: once again, the question was about the relationship between culture and power, that is, hegemony—which was what kept getting in the way in the Indian and Brazilian stories.

In Terni, I was a native member of the community, and my oral history work was rooted in my rank-and-file connections;

in Appalachia, over the course of thirty years of research visits, and thanks to good introductions, I also gathered first-hand narratives from coal miners and community members. In both places, I was conversant with the language and the history of the place. In the cases of Brazil and India, however, there was a different relationship. The Brazilian interviews were done by others, with a whole different approach; the conversation in India took place across a linguistic barrier, mediated by a competent and participant interpreter, Abhivyakti's Anita Borkar, and yet sufficient to prevent me from going deeper into the narratives (also, I always preferred the intensity of one-on-one to group interviews). More importantly, the Brazilian interviews had been commissioned by the company itself, and the speakers were middle-range technicians, managers, a few elite skilled workers; in Igatpuri, the longest interview (in a shared language) took place with the personnel manager, while a group interview with workers (chosen by management) took place in the personnel office in the presence of a sympathetic but watchful management representative. In these cases, then, the stories I heard were mediated not only by linguistic difference (I can at least read Portuguese) but by power relationships: if there was an alternative history in the oral 'testimony' I was hearing, it would have to be glimpsed through the lines of the controlled narratives I was given. And that would have required a linguistic analysis in a language I didn't know.

At our first meeting, an Abhivyakti staff member told a story of great methodological significance for the politics of oral history. Recently, he said, there was a clash between the police and landless workers, in which two demonstrators were killed. At the inquest, all the witnesses on the side of the landlords told exactly the same story in the same words (clearly, they had been instructed and carefully rehearsed), while the witnesses on the side of the workers told spontaneously a myriad of stories that varied in point of view, in details, in language, in emotional and political impact. The result was that the court could not reach a final conclusion and draw a unified reconstruction of the event, and was unable to pass a verdict. The lesson of the story, we agreed, was that it's always the power structure that tries to force one single narrative on the complexity of historical experience, while the power of the non-hegemonic narratives lies in their plurality and multiplicity. Which is what oral history is largely about, and was mainly missing in the controlled narratives from Belo Horizonte and Igatpuri.

Two days before the interviews in Igatpuri, Anita Borkar and Nitin Paranjape, with other members of Abhivyakti, showed me a piece of land that they had just bought. It looked like a yellow desert of gilded hills like elephants, steeples and painted plains. You should see it in the rainy season, they explained, when it is all green. In the distance, on the horizon, I could see the abandoned sheds of what had been conceived as Asia's largest industrial development area. The whole plan collapsed after costing outlandish amounts of money; but it left its mark on the landscape. Along the Nashik road run the pipelines that take water to the industrial zone, bypassing the dry villages along the way.

Nitin and Anita invested all their money (with some help from Arundhati Roy), to create on this land a centre of 'local learning': building on the knowledge, the skills, the trades created along the centuries by the local communities and villages in order to develop alternative ways of survival. I admire the small dams made of rocks and stones across the gullies to control and collect water. There must be a dozen deep wells, some finished some underway; the earth and stone recovered from the excavation are reused to fix or erect buildings. Here, indeed, I become aware of the meaning of water.

I try not to wax romantic about it all, and ask myself: would I live here? Maybe not. Later in the day we return to Dhondegaon. The ladies I had met the year before remember and welcome me. Proudly, one of them, called Kale, shows me the latest development: a compost bed they are creating to generate organic fertilizer. In order to make it more productive, they will seed the earth with earthworms, which chew and digest the earth and make it more fertile (and, as the earthworms reproduce, they can sell them to other villages for additional income). Where do you get the earthworms?, I ask. 'From us,' says Nitin: the cooperative raises them in a box they keep in their office. Abhivyakti produces both film and earthworms: agri/culture, indeed.

Kale says that more and more families are returning to biological agriculture, which may be less productive in the short run but saves the land from destruction. I am reminded of a passage in the autobiography of Luigi Stifani, the musician from Salento who played the violin to heal the 'tarantate,' rural women who experienced a historical 'loss of presence,' a sense of inadequacy in the face of the incredible odds they faced in the lives, as a crisis of possession they believe to be caused by the bite of a mythical spider (called 'taranta,' from which 'tarantella,' the traditional dance that resolves the trance and restores balance and order). The dance ritual, Stifani wrote in his second-grade spelling and lettering, is disappearing, because the fields have been poisoned with so many chemicals that the all living creatures, including the imaginary spiders, have died.

People are still suffering, the crisis and the pain have changed but are as real as ever, and we have lost the ritual that helped deal with them.

I don't perceive much pain, at this place and time, however. Of course they are very poor. The compost, the worms, the few ears of wheat that Kale's husband gathers to roast the seeds on the open fire and offer them to us—it's as if they were carefully scratching the surface of the planet to use and reuse every small thing they can. Yet, poverty is one thing, and the misery I have seen in the streets of the city is another. They are poor, but they do not beg, they give: tea, the peanuts they grew themselves, the roasted seeds, two plastic chairs for the guests (especially the westerner, who is too stiff to squat comfortably on the ground). They sit and stand straight, wear colored saris and glistening rings on their fingers. The animals lie placidly on the ground only a few steps away.

When the folks at Abhivyakti asked me whether the closing of a factory is such a terrible thing, they were probably thinking of such scenes. The scene might have been more or less the same a hundred years ago (except the plastic chairs for the outsiders), but it does not feel like a plunge out of history—rather, like being back to square one to what might be the start of a different history, a different way of life. Not a paradise (how would I survive, with no electricity to read and write, without internet access...) but not without meaning. Not without pain, either—else, why should the 'tarantate' dance?

Ernesto De Martino called the lands of Salento where they lived 'le Indie di quaggiù', our own Indies—a place as alien, and distant from mainstream Italian culture as the actual lands and people of the Far East or the Caribbean, and as 'pagan' and poor as them (Carlo Levi had written, in an earlier classic memoir, that Christ Stopped at Eboli, just south of Naples, leaving these lands and people outside the pale of Western, European history). And yet, far from being outside history, perhaps they are part a different history, and I am the one who is left out. Perhaps, I am the one who is on the wrong historical track, or at least a separate one, and the work of oral history is the work of trying to join these histories together as one. As Ernesto deMartino wrote after exploring and learning 'the Indias of down here,' the people that live there are not aliens, but 'citizens of [our] own country' (p. 3), partners in the search for a shared history, and our task is to try to stand together, steel workers in Terni and Igatpuri, rural women in Dhondegaon and Salento, and us scholars and activists, citizens of the same world, in a shared history and future.

ThyssenKrupp, Terni, Umbria, Italy

In January, 2004, the workers at the ThyssenKrupp (TK) steel plant in Terni, Umbria, in Central Italy, went on strike. ThyssenKrupp, the German conglomerate that had taken over the factory after it was privatised from state ownership in 1994, had announced that it would close the magnetic steel department and other sectors of the factory. At least 900 jobs were in jeopardy.

As soon as the news reached them at the plant, the workers stopped production and marched to the Garden Hotel, where TK representatives were announcing their decision to the unions, the city mayor and the region's administrators. Lucia Rossi, then secretary of Terni's labour exchange remembers: 'The workers broke into the room, and there was a melee because the workers started tossing whatever they could lay hands on. There was pastry, cakes, on the table, and they began to throw them every which way, I still remember [Ada] Girolamini, the regional secretary for economic development, with custard all over her hair…'

It was the beginning of a month-long struggle. The workers, the unions, the town saw the threatened closing of the magnetic steel division as a harbinger of the closing of the whole factory. While it had lost some of its centrality and had been reduced in size, the steel factory was still the core of Terni's economy and identity, as it had been since it was first established in 1885. Thus, the town responded with huge demonstrations (30,000 people marching in 2004 out of a population of less than 100,000), picket lines, road blocks, occupation of the railroad, total solidarity. After two months of sustained struggle, ThyssenKrupp went back on its decision, the magnetic steel division and the jobs at risk were saved.

A year later, TK was back on the warpath. This time it managed to close the magnetic steel division and, although no jobs were lost, the loss of its cutting-edge production was perceived by most workers and townspeople as a serious blow to the economy and identity of the town and its factory. But this story takes us back to a year before, the spring of 2004.

ThyssenKrupp, Igatpuri, Maharashtra, India

In March 2004, a few weeks after Terni's general strike, I was driving by Igatpuri, near Nashik, on the mountains behind Mumbai, India, when a sign on a factory gate caught my eye: 'EBG India Electrical Steel. A ThyssenKrupp company.' I had never seen globalisation at such close quarters. The workers in Terni hardly knew about the existence of a sister plant (or is it a competitor?) in India; the Igatpuri security personnel with whom I managed to exchange a few words by the factory gate had never heard of Terni. In globalisation, power is unified, while workers are divided and know little or nothing about one another.

A year later, with the help of Abhivyakti (a local cooperative for alternative media and rural development), I was able to conduct some interviews in the factory. Mr. Somendra Pal, head of human resources:

> OK, I'll tell you. The company was set up in 1995, ten years ago. That time it was part of another group called Raymond in India, and they are into textile basically they make woolen garments. Since it was not part of their core business, they could not run it properly and it was running into heavy losses. So they started looking for a buyer. In the year 2000, the Thyssen group bought it. That time it was known as EBG India and it was bought by Thyssen group in September, 2000. It's a 100 percent core subsidiary of this group. Our managing director is German, nominated by the Group, and another full time director is a German. [It made] electrical steel and mild steel both, from the beginning. We have our Board of Directors, including some people from Germany and some local Indian people.

The company employs 710 men and 10 women (in secretarial jobs); about 500 are blue collar (skilled machine operators 'are blue collar but we call them white collar'). 'ThyssenKrupp has five units in India' that make auto parts (Pune, Chennai) or elevators (Delhi); Igatpuri is, however, the only one that makes electric steel, 'for electrical applications like motors and starters and transformers. Right now there is tremendous shortage of steel worldwide, so we are having tremendous opportunity of selling everywhere, domestic, export, everywhere'.

So how come TK was shutting the magnetic steel division in Terni? 'It's a different matter. I don't know the entire story, I only know a little bit of it. There were several issues connected with quality of production', Pal explained. Terni was 'a different matter. As far as I know, it was a problem with the quality of the product.' Terni's workers claim that they make the best steel (and especially magnetic steel) in the world, and are proud of their skill and work ethics; yet, ThyssenKrupp was telling its Indian executives that the problems there were caused by the low quality of the product. I ask Mr Pal if he had ever been in Terni: 'I have visited ThyssenKrupp plants in France and Germany, but they advised me not to go to Terni. They'll break your legs if you go there. You arrive on your own legs, but may not be able to walk out on them.' The echo of the invasion of the Garden Hotel and the day of the flying cakes had traveled all the way to this air-conditioned office in India.

'In 2003, the Communists came, with a big crowd at the gates: they wanted a union. We didn't let them in. We pushed them back. The law in Maharashtra allows the workers to create company unions, so now we have a company union and relations are peaceful' said Somendra Pal. 'We had contacted a Communist union,' a worker said, 'but the company said they would never recognise it, so we decided to have an in-house union that the company would be willing to recognize. Relations are good, I have no reason to think of quitting' (Rajesh).[1]

ThyssenKrupp does not recognise the workers' right to chose their own union, but secures their fidelity through traditional paternalistic practices: hiring the sons of workers who retire, as the company used to do in Terni until a couple of generation ago. About 100 workers who come from other communities live in a 'residential colony inside the plant' and can shop at a company store, according to Somendra Pal.

Labour relations include sports events, and public dialogue between workers and management: 'Each year the company calls a meeting of all employees to listen to what we have to say about the work, our grievances, and we discuss it all together' (Nisar). Paternalism also extends to the community: every year, together with other German companies, TK organises an event called 'Nashik run', to raise money for community issues and donate to the Red Cross and hospitals (Anita, my friend from Abhivyakti who accompanies me and will later act as interpret, rolls her eyes—'they have no idea of what the reality is like,' she comments, afterwards).

Good relations

The function of paternalism is, of course, to deflect industrial conflict and to create friendly, 'trouble-free' relations between management and 'the boys'. Pal said:

> Labor relations so far—touch wood—have been very good, have been extremely good. In this area, lots of companies had to close down due to union trouble. Dr. Karak, the Communist guy. Lots of units had to close because of him. Lots of companies closed down because of the fear of the union. Dr. Karak is trying to come here also. He brought a big crowd at the gate and wanted to enter the plant in here. We did not let him come in. We have a union which is affiliated to a national organisation called INTUC [Indian National Trade Union Congress] and the boys are members of that.

After my interview with the manager, I talked to a group of workers—in the presence of another human relations manager. One of them, a union steward, explained that 'We never had a strike because the atmosphere between the management and the union is very happy.' Talking all at once and interrupting one another, the workers explain that they had indeed thought of calling Mr D. L. Karad (not his real name) and his Communist union; 'but the management did not support us in this matter'. So they joined another, Mumbai-based union, but it was unsatisfactory: 'the people got fed up as the person running the union was in Mumbai and did not listen to the grievances of the people. The company did not want [the Communist union], we didn't want [this other union] so we thought of choosing a middle path' and form their own company union, which management promptly recognised, so that they would deal with their own problems themselves and not have to pay dues to an outside organisation.

They had heard about Terni—'was it because of union problems? It can't happen here, because of the production we make, and the good relations between workers and management' (Ravi). I reminded them that the workers had been saying exactly the same things in Terni before the crisis—good production, social peace, friendly labour relations... and they seemed concerned. They know that a multinational company's strategy overrules and ignores the details of local conditions.

Generations of workers

The stories these workers told me were those of the first generations of industrial workers—very different from those of their contemporaries in Terni, but not unlike those of Terni's first generations.

Indeed, Terni and Igatpuri seemed to be at the opposite ends of the industrial revolution: Terni at its end, Igatpuri at the beginning. Like early generations of Terni workers, Igatpuri workers had memories of the land; some worked in the factory to help their families back at the village; they didn't necessarily dislike industrial work but had memories of another way of life and work, so they do not take factory work for granted: 'Working in the open air is good. Indoor work is hard. We have to follow the rules as given by management. We have to follow the boss's orders and heed his words, no matter how hard you work.' Even when they like factory work better than farming, as a worker named Prabhakar Rambhan says, their identity is still rooted on the land: 'We are farmers first, our forefathers were farmers. My parents too were farmers. My wife works [on the land]'; a co-worker sitting near him comments: 'He likes [the land] because it's an ancestral thing.' 'Farming pulls at my heart strings', another says.

To some, a factory job is a way of maintaining the land: 'We still work the land when we go back. [I came to work here because] I thought that, along with farming, joining the factory would be an additional income, which I would use for cultivating the land.' To others, it's a necessity (often a welcome one) because the land could no longer support their growing families: 'We are happy here. We are adequately provided for, and so we can maintain our family well. If the company was not there, we would have to do farming, where our income would not have been sufficient. Our children are getting an education because of the company. The children have become smarter than us.'

'I come from a village nearby. My family works the land. Part of our land has been bought by the company, and part of it is still ours, my wife works on it. I've been working here for ten years, since the factory started. I used to like working the land. I don't mind the work here, but it's boring. I'll be here until I retire' (Ravi). A man I am calling Rajesh explained that he was studying art in college, but his family's land was confiscated to build the dam that supplied power to the factory; the compensation they received was negligible, but since the law required the company to hire at least 5 per cent of its work force from 'project-affected families', he applied and was hired. He never finished college. 'I come from a rural background, a rural family. I grew up in the village, then I came to Nashik to learn to be a mechanic. I worked at a number of jobs, then I was hired here. My family has moved to Nashik but we still own the land in the village and we go for ceremonies, religious holidays, family events. I don't know what I will do in the future but I think I'll go back to the village. I feel that I have an organic relation to the earth, like the blood relation I have with my siblings. If you work the land, you are directed by your family; here, you must take orders from strangers' (Sharad).

> I am Varun Dhasan. Age 26 years. My village is in Malegaon. It's a small village. I came to Nashik to study in the seventh class. I studied till class 10; I got tired of studying in English medium, I failed English and I went home. I was happy at home. I used to go to the farm land, the orchards, the banana plantations, the sugarcane fields. I was very happy. We had a tractor at home. I was sixteen years old. I used to ride that tractor every day, go out in the morning and come back in the evening. I was enjoying life.

His family, however, sent him back to town and got him a job in the factory so that he could help the family with his wages:

> I came to work here because of the pressure from my family, but I ran away and went back to work in the fields. I didn't like the idea of being here and doing always the same job, I wanted to do something different, something exciting, and working in the fields seemed different from everything else. But my family forced me to go back to school, a vocational school—I didn't like it

> but I had to finish. And I was hired here as an apprentice. I ran away again, and again my family sent me back; now I finished my apprenticeship, I'm here and I don't like it at all. We had a deal in the family, that one male child would go away to work [to earn monetary income for the family], and I was the one. Yet we had agreed that if I didn't like the work I'd go back home. Now I don't mind the work here, but I guess sooner or later I'll run away again and go home.

Global Steel

'ThyssenKrupp is a multinational conglomerate of 670 companies, almost 200,000 employees, and 45 offices all over the world.' (Novelli et al, 64–65) The data and figures of globalisation are one thing; another thing is bumping into it everywhere you go: the 'fingers' that connect the terminal to the plane at Sao Paolo airport in Brazil, the escalators in the Oslo subway (and, I am told, in Riyadh, Saudi Arabia), the elevator at the Brescia railway station, the giant crane in the Capetown harbour (my friends at Witwatersrand University tried in vain to interview the South African TK workers in Johannesburg), the elevator in a cheap motel in Logan Country, West Virginia or in a Holiday Inn in Lexington, Kentucky—all bear the ThyssenKrupp name. Martina Canali, a young woman from Terni who has lived and travelled all over Europe, confirms: 'Whenever I travel around the world and I see the words, ThyssenKrupp, on the ground, on the elevators, I think, look, these bastards, wherever I go there they are.'

In 2010 I tried to start an international oral history project on ThyssenKrupp workers. We failed to get funding, and the only place where it was brought to completion was Brazil.[2] At the time, ThyssenKrupp owned or controlled 22 companies in Brazil, with 13,000 employees, from auto parts in Sao Paulo and Minas Gerais to elevators in Porto Alegre.[3] An e-mail from Paulinho Almeida from the University of Uberlandia (Minas Gerais), one of the project's coordinators, explained[4]:

> Many times in my life have I heard people say, 'Working at ThyssenKrupp is the dream of all the metal workers in the greater Sao Paulo region. When I taught high school, many students dropped out of school to take vocational courses with a dream of one day going to work for Krupp. Often, in the days of political activism, we demonstrated at the factory gates, and there was a rejection of the union because they all wanted to work here. Krupp started a tradition of training their employees' children so they could go to work for the company.

The history of Krupp in Brazil goes back to 1837; that of Thyssen, to 1908. Paulinho Almeida adds: 'There are rumours that Krupp had established itself in the area to produce weapons for World War II. But it was only an assembly plant, so the workers didn't know what they were doing because pieces were assembled separately in a huge industrial park and there was no communication among the workers in different shifts and divisions. These are the stories you hear. Much later, they specialised in auto parts for Brazil and Argentina.'

Like in India, ThyssenKrupp in Brazil stands as a major modern industrial complex in a formerly rural environment. Thus, as in Igatpuri, it practices a careful policy of fidelisation, often in continuity with previous management of companies it has taken over. Gisela Marins, who worked at an elevator plant that later became ThyssenKrupp in Porto Alegre, and has relatives still employed in it, remembers:

> The company is a part of your personal life and your personal life is a continuation of the life of the company. In this factory at Porto Alegre, for instance, they have a center where employees

> can organise parties for their children, playgrounds and sports fields, a whole structure so that in your leisure time you can keep going back to the company with your family. The factory as family.[5]

The same is true for the auto parts plant at Ibirité, Minais Gerais, a supplier of the Fiat plant at Belo Horizonte: the *gremio* (the employees association) 'always organised New Year's Eve parties. We sang and played the *batuque* ourselves. The New Year's Eve party was sacred, we all took our families. We had soccer tournaments, each division had its own team, I played left midfielder for Maintenance. We won almost every year' (Januário Cosme Damião).[6]

'The ThyssenKrupp model is the German model, harsh, structured, square, and here we have our *jetinho*, 'our little way' of doing things Brazilian style. In the end, we proved that the firm's success was not a coincidence, but was the fruit of a work in which everybody takes part' (Lázaro de Figueredo Júnior). At another ThyssenKrupp plant in Minas Gerais, management tried to ban the use of the word 'trabalhadores' (workers) and replace it with 'colaboradores' (collaborators); the workers were not pleased (Morais, 211–240). The Brazilian *jeitinho* at Ibirité has much in common with the ThyssenKrupp model at Igatpuri in India: 'coffee with the boss,' 'megaphone sessions' in which workers can voice their ideas and complaints; and the time-honored practice of hiring their own workers' children: 'When a father brings in his son and then in turn the son brings in his own, and now we have generations that have been working here, this is the sign of a serious commitment toward the company' (Lázaro de Figueredo Júnior). The policy of paternalism, again as in Igatpuri, is functional to countering the rise of the unions.

> At Ibirité we found out that at the Fiat plant [in Belo Horizonte, Minas Gerais] they hire no one unless they have a letter of recommendation from someone who is already working there. We realized also that at Fiat there were no strikes and that since they had adopted this philosophy they had doubled productivity and reduced work accidents. We introduced this system in the plant at Ibirité, and today we rely on it very much (Eduardo Bertolini).

October 2005. On the road between Hopkinsville and Shelbyville, not far from Louisville, Kentucky, behind a row of trees, a sign on a factory gate: ThyssenKrupp Budd, an automotive part supplier. A few months earlier, in February, 2005, while Terni was again on strike over the magnetic steel plant, the ThyssenKrupp Budd union contract expired: 'ThyssenKrupp Budd asked workers for $10 million in concessions, including cutting pay by $5 an hour, a $160-a-month increase in health insurance premiums, and elimination of retiree health care benefits and cost-of-living adjustments.' (Adams) The workers struck, and, under pressure from its customers for deliveries, the company caved in and the contract was renewed without concessions. In 2006 ThyssenKrupp sold all its 13 automotive body and chassis operations in North America to Martinrea International Inc.; as a consequence, at least fifty workers at the Shelbyville plant were laid off.[7]

'On 11 May 2007, ThyssenKrupp AG announced an investment of €3.1 billion (US$4.19 billion) for a project consisting of building new carbon steel and stainless steel processing facilities in southern Alabama that would employ 2,700 people when fully operational. The project, along with a multibillion-dollar steelmaking facility in Brazil, was a cornerstone of ThyssenKrupp's global expansion strategy into the North American and NAFTA high-value carbon steel markets. The company announced that the investment was increased to $4.6 billion in 2010. As of the date of the announcement, the investment was the largest private economic development investment in Alabama's history and the largest by a German company in the U.S.'[8] Alabama was chosen because it offered 'tax breaks for everything from utility payments to capital costs,' a nearly total exemption from corporate income tax, and 'substantial cash from Mobile city and county governments' for an expected 100 million dollars.[9] And, of course, no unions.

The company announced that it would employ 29,000 workers in construction and 2,700 once production was on the way. Among the enthusiastic comments of local bloggers and politicians, some were more doubtful: 'I'm excited about the plant, but I have a math problem. The 26,000 construction jobs seem to end in 2010. The 2700 factory jobs are great, but a 90% reduction in work-force. Am I missing something? Where do the other 23,000 workers go?'[10] In fact, not even all the 2,700 who will stay to run the plant would be local; many might even come from Terni:

> They are asking some of the boys if they'd like to go to America to work, because of course if they have people who are already qualified it gives them a head start. Some might actually go. It's a matter of economic convenience, and there are so many things involved. I mean, nowadays America is here, not there, the Euro is the dollar. Yet, some young man might say: I work there for ten years, make 60,000 Euros instead of 20,000, save some money, maybe buy a home or something... (Pietro Marcelli).

The 2008 economic crisis changed it all. The economic feasibility of Thyssen Krupp's Alabama plant was founded on imported steel slabs from its plant in Brazil; the plan however fell apart because of the recession and increasing production costs in Brazil. Between 2013 and 2014, the plant was parceled out, at a loss, to the Finnish company Outokompo and to a joint venture between Indian conglomerate Arcelor and Japan's Nippon Steel and Sumitomo Metal. At the time, the plant employed 1,600 workers, less than 60 per cent of the vaunted 2,700 jobs. None came from Terni (Nelson-Gabriel).

The Quality of Chinese Steel

Global steel generates a deep change in the mentality of the workers. Terni's steelworkers had long basked in a sort of exceptionalism: they were the oldest and only large industrial site in Central Italy, and the geographical position of the town—in a valley basin surrounded by mountains—reinforced their feeling of separation and identity. Also, the fact that the factory had been state-owned since the 1930s contributed to this feeling of difference. The ThyssenKrupp acquisition, and the world trend of globalisation changed their mentality, their language and their world view. The change was also reinforced by immigration. For generations, Terni's steelworkers had been local people (though part of the first generation in the 1880s had migrated southwards from Romagna); nowadays, the lower, unskilled contract jobs in the plant are performed also by migrants from Southern Italy, and from Romania, Morocco, or India. Krishna Kumar from Bihar, India, explains:

> When I came to Italy [in 2005] it was hard to find a job because I didn't know the language, so I stayed home for five or six months, then I enrolled at the vocational school, to study the Italian language. [He did occasional jobs, then was hired as a temporary worker by a TK contractor and, in 2008, he finally obtained a regular contract.] In 2010, my daughter Surbi was

> born. All the time when I'm home she eats with me, sleeps with me, plays with me, she likes to do everything with me, I'm always with my daughter. But even though she was born here, she doesn't have Italian citizenship. Maybe later, when she's 18, she can apply for citizenship, and we will see what happens then.[11]

February 26, 2005. Terni was again on strike and marching in defense of steel mill jobs. Over a glass of wine, young steel worker Emanuele Albi and some of his colleagues discussed globalisation, strategies, policies, institutions. Some of the comments were so general as to risk abstraction; others were rooted in the here and now. These young workers were fiercely critical of local institutions, unions included; and though their working-class professional pride was still the backbone of their identity, yet their vision was no longer restricted to the exceptionalist perspective of Terni's valley basin, but included an awareness of the worldwide context and the global dimensions of what was happening to their town. They still spoke with the local accent and used vernacular idioms, yet their language now included all sorts of contemporary anglicised globalspeak. The new global language first entered the discourse of sports, leisure, entertainment, music; but it quickly became also part of the lexicon of factory, work and union: English words like *corporate, core business, board, controller, stainless, coil, step, revamp* may still be declined with a Terni accent, but are used competently and appropriately, a clear signal of a change in perspective.

They had the data on production, market quotas, industrial policies at their fingertips. Being productive is no longer enough; now workers must come to terms with market problems, company policy, global context ('our steel,' says one, 'is being finished in China'). A worker from the pipe mill division complained that 'to a multinational, Terni is a drop in the ocean'; a comrade replied that, on the contrary, it is a link in a chain that would break without them: 'We make 15 per cent of muffler pipes for the European auto industry. If we stop, Renault stops, Volvo breaks down.'

Fragments of a conversation between workers of different generations.

> *Nevio Brunori*: We used to make rough stainless steel rolls and send them to Mexico and China to be finished there, or Brazil. Nowadays in China they're building a plant that can produce 9 million tons of steel a year. China only needs three million for its internal market.
>
> *Marco Allegretti*: Yes, but don't you know that China had to throw away several tons of steel because it wasn't up to European standards? Do you really think that China can really make quality steel? I mean, once you've saturated the home market, how are you going to sell it abroad?
>
> *Nevio Brunori*: Listen, do you still believe that Terni steel is good because of the quality of our water?[12] What you're talking about was true for magnetic steel. Magnetic steel, you must make it beautiful inside, not just outside. It must be beautiful inside, for what it serves. Stainless steel, as long as it's shiny on the outside, it's all right. If you can do the rough product, it can be finished and shined afterwards.
>
> *Marco Allegretti*: But that's not the only kind of steel there is; steel also goes into the infrastructures, and for that it needs to have certain characteristics. The market of steel has changed, it's been liberalized, the competition is so tough that any kind of steel you make must be good both inside and outside. The Chinese can make shiny steel all right, but if it isn't good inside they can't sell much of it.
>
> *Emanuele Albi*: The rolls we send out are used for kitchen sinks, for forks, and such; now there is a whole range of low-quality

products that it is all brought in from China, it's made with steel shiny outside, because anyone can make that. What he's talking about, the infrastructures, is forged steel, magnetic steel, and to make these things it takes...

Nevio Brunori: The stainless steel we make in Terni isn't meant for big infrastructures, we don't make steel construction beams. What we make is laminates; and nowadays, those rolls we used to send to China and Mexico, they can make them themselves. So let me tell you: China has a surplus of 9 million tons of [that kind] of steel.

Marco Allegretti: You know, nowadays Terni accounts for two percent of all ThyssenKrupp sales. If China begins to invest in quality....

What's normal about a factory?

As we leave the plant in Igatpuri, Anita Borkar comments: 'Did you see the noise, in there, the heat, an all-male environment—and they call it a good life!' A rural activist, this is her first visit to a factory. Later, I give a talk about the struggle in Terni to the rural activists of Abhivyakti. At the end, the first question chills me: 'Is it such a bad thing if a factory closes?'

Such a question would never have been asked in Terni, at least until a generation ago, when industrialisation was still perceived as the wave of the future (and the industrial working class the vanguard of social change). De-industrialisation and globalisation on the one hand, and the memory of rural culture and life, change the perspective: the factory is no longer and not yet taken for granted. Anita Borkar's question was a perfect case of what literary theorists call 'estrangement': the familiar seen with unfamiliar eyes, and suddenly revealed in all its absurdity. Anita called attention both to the social 'all-male' environment, and to the physical environment. Indeed, younger workers in

Terni no longer see a factory job as their ideal, and no longer accept as easily the work environment and the working conditions that their parents and grandparents took for granted: 'Just last week, we stopped everything and came down from the gantry crane where we were working because we couldn't breathe. We dropped everything, left the work unfinished, we came down, told the maintenance manager that either he found a way for us to work in safety up there, or the work remained undone' (Luciano Berni).[13]

Even more radical is the change of perspective in terms of the factory's impact on the surrounding environment. As industrial jobs become fewer, and their contribution in terms of income and employment ebbs, environmental awareness rises. In Nashik, this awareness was reinforced by the commitment to a rural culture and way of life; in Terni, people for over a century breathed the fumes and dust from the factory, and accepted it as an inevitable price—indeed, sometimes a proud symbol—of work and progress. Today, many see the factory as much as a threat to the environment as a creator of wealth and jobs. So, while I perceived the closing of the steel mills as a tragedy for working people, others saw it as a possible boon for the environment. Emanuele Salvati, a young steel worker and activist explains:

> We have a big environmental problem. We have a deep affection for the working class and its history, but cannot pretend we do not see that there is a huge open-air dump, that Terni is the most polluted town in Umbria, that we are going through an environmental crisis that the unions and the town always refused to recognise and to deal with. This might be an opportunity to reconcile the people of Terni, because a part of the town would like the factory to close, because it is reduced in size, is no longer as useful and necessary as it used to be, a source of

> income and a living for so many families, but rather a health, environmental problem. So if we faced up to it we might try to reconcile working conditions with the environmental awareness, which has grown very much in Terni in recent times.[14]

The question asked by the young activist reveals an even more complex perspective in that it denotes both a pre-industrial and a post-industrial dimension. It is a remark that encompasses the past, the present and the future. On the one hand, it refers to a still-living, pre-industrial heritage, a culture still alive in the first-generation Igatpuri workers who retained links to the land, or even wished to go back to it. On the other hand, it expresses a contemporary environmental awareness, and the sense that there must be alternatives to the all-pervasive hegemony of industrial economy and culture. So these few words helped me recognise how the history of the rise and fall of the factory in Terni, in the brief span of about one hundred years, suggests that the Industrial Revolution has only been a transitory, ephemeral passage in the history of mankind. There was a world before the factory, and hopefully there's a world after it loses its central position in our lives and imagination.

Epilogue

In 2014, ThyssenKrupp sold the Terni factory to a Finnish conglomerate, Outokompo. The sale, however, was voided by the European government, because it would have upset competition in steel making. TK had to take back the plant, but it had now become a sort of unwanted white elephant. In 2015, the company announced a cut of 400 employees in its work force. The workers responded with a three-month strike, one of the longest in Italian labour history. At the end, however, four hundred workers accepted a bonus and resigned individually from their factory jobs. Like the workers who were fired en masse in 1953 and used their severance pay to start small businesses, some successful, some not, these workers will probably use their bonuses to finish paying for the apartments they bought on debt, or invest in some other enterprise.

In October 2019, after fifteen years of tough labour struggles that ended in defeat, compromise and a sharply reduced factory employment, the once solid-red town of Terni voted 55.7 per cent for the extreme right. Perhaps the closing of a factory is not such a liberation after all. There is no chance that any of the workers who gave up their jobs will go back to working the land.

Notes

1. A pseudonym. Most of the the Igatpuri workers asked me not to use their names.
2. The project was coordinated by Prof. Yara Khouri of the Catholic University of Sao Paulo and Prof. Paulo Almeida, of the Federal University of Uberlandia. See Khoury, pp. 1–13. http://www.snh2011.anpuh.org/resources/anais/14/1308167312_ARQUIVO_COMUNICACAO_ANPUH_Yara_Aun_Khoury.pdf. see July 23, 2016.
3. 'ThyssenKrupp in Brazil,' http://thyssenkrupp-steel.com/csa/en/brazilien, retrieved June 26, 2008. This page is no longer available.
4. Paulo Almeida, professor of social history at the University of Uberlandia (Minas Gerais), e-mail, June 25, 2008.
5. Gisele Marins, a cultural worker for the Brazilian Embassy in Rome, was interviewed in Rome, June 5, 2012
6. The Ibirité interviews were recorded by the Museo da Pessoa in Sao Paulo, on commission from ThyssenKrupp.
7. 'ThyssenKrupp Budd to sell North American automotive body operations.' http://americanmachinist.com/uncategorized/thyssenkrupp-budd-sell-north-american-automotive-body-operations; 'About

50 workers expected to lose jobs at Martinrea plant,' March 13, 2008, http://www.bizjournals.com/louisville/stories/2008/03/17/story7.html, both retrieved July 23, 2016.

8. https://en.wikipedia.org/wiki/ThyssenKrupp, retrieved July 23, 2016.
9. https://www.google.it/?client=firefox-b#q=mobile+county+wins+thyssenkrupp+plant&gfe_rd=c, retrieved July 23, 2016: 'The new plant would have to make over $2.8 billion a year from a $3.7 billion plant [...]before it paid any corporate income taxes. Media reports put ThyssenKrupp's 2006 profit at slightly under $3.4 billion -- meaning the new plant would have to produce 82 percent of ThyssenKrupp's company-wide profit before paying corporate income taxes to Alabama.'
10. Ibid., comment signed '26point2.'
11. Interviewed in Greca Campus, *Lotta senza classe* (2014), https://vimeo.com/108579387.
12. He alludes to the belief that it's the quality of the water that makes Naples coffee the best in the world.
13. Luciano Berni, steel worker, b. 1959, 2.6.2004.
14. Emanuele Salvati, steel worker, b.1977), 11.5.2016.

References

Adams, B. 2005. 'ThyssenKrupp Budd workers Reach Tentative Agreement.' *Business First*, Louisville (KY), Feb. 9, http://www.bizjournals.com/louisville/stories/2005/02/07/daily24.html, retrieved July 23, 2016.

Campus, Greca. 2014. *Lotta senza classe*. https://vimeo.com/108579387.

Khoury, Yara Aun. 2011. 'A empresa ThyssenKrupp do Brasil e seus Trabalhadores: A problemática da memória come linguagem social e prática política', A*nais do XXVI Simpósio Nacional de História—ANPUH*. São Paulo, July, pp. 1–13.

Martino, Ernesto de. 1959. 'Etnologia e cultura nazionale negli ultii dieci anni'. *Società*, IX, p. 3.

Morais, Sergio Paulo 2016. 'Memórias em disputa: globalisaçao, trabalho industrial e pautas sindacais (1990–2015). *História e Perspectivas*, Uberlândia (Minas Gerais), 55, July–December, 2016, pp. 211–240.

Nelson-Gabriel, Melissa. 2013. 'Massive Thyssenkrupp steel plant in Calvert being sold for an estimated $1.55 billion,' *The Associated Press*. Dec. 26. http://www.tuscaloosanews.com/article/20131226/NEWS/131229821, retrieved 23 July 2016.

Novelli, D et al. 2008. *ThyssenKrupp. L'inferno della classe operaia*. Mila: Sperling & Kupfer, pp. 64–5.

Pal, Somendra. 2006. Personal interviews. 14 March.

Rossi, Lucia. 2008. Personal communication, 16 February.

Viscardi, Giuseppe Maria. 2005. *Tra Europa e 'Indie di quaggiù'*, Roma, Edizioni di Sto ria e Letteratura.

What Makes Oral History Different

This article, first published in 1979, challenged oral history's critics head-on by arguing that 'what makes oral history different'—orality, narrative form, subjectivity, the 'different credibility' of memory, and the relationship between interviewer and interviewee—should be considered as strengths rather than as weaknesses, a resource rather than a problem. Alessandro Portelli holds a Chair in American Literature at the University of Rome. Reprinted by permission from *The Death* of *Luigi Trastulli and Other Stories: Form and Meaning in Oral History* by Alessandro Portelli, the State University of New York Press A first version, 'Sulla specificita della storia orale', appeared in *Primo Maggio* (Milano, Italy), 1979, vol. 13, pp. 54–60, reprinted as 'On the peculiarities of oral history' in *History Workshop Journal,* 1981, no. 12, pp. 96–107.

> 'Yes,' said Mrs. Oliver, 'and then when they come to talk about it a long time afterwards, they've got the solution for it which they've made up themselves. That isn't awfully helpful, is it?' 'It is helpful,' said Poirot ... 'It's important to know certain facts which have lingered in people's memories although they may not know exactly what the fact was, why it happened or what led to it. But they might easily know something that we do not know and that we have no means of learning. So there have been memories leading to theories.'
>
> Agatha Christie, *Elephants Can Remember*

His historical researches, however, did not lie so much among books as among men; for the former are lamentably scanty on his favorite topics; whereas he found the old burghers, and still more their wives, rich in that legendary lore, so invaluable to true history. Whenever, therefore, he happened upon a genuine

> Dutch family, snugly shut up in its low-roofed farmhouse, under a spreading sycamore, he looked upon it as a little clasped volume of black-letter and studied it with the zeal of a book-worm.
>
> Washington Irving, 'Rip Van Winkle'

Memories leading to theories

A specter is haunting the halls of the academy: the specter of oral history. The Italian intellectual community, always suspicious of news from outside and yet so subservient to 'foreign discoveries'—hastened to cut oral history down to size before even trying to understand what it is and how to use it. The method used has been that of charging oral history with pretensions it does not have, in order to set everybody's mind at ease by refuting them. For instance, *La Repubblica,* the most intellectually and internationally oriented of Italian dailies rushed to dismiss 'descriptions "from below" and the artificial packages of "oral history" where things are supposed to move and talk by themselves', without even stopping to notice that it is not *things*, but *people* (albeit people often considered no more than 'things') that oral history expects to 'move and talk by themselves'.[1]

There seems to be a fear that once the floodgates of orality are opened, writing (and rationality along with it) will be swept out as if by a spontaneous uncontrollable mass of fluid, amorphous material. But this attitude blinds us to the fact that our awe of writing has distorted our perception of language and communication to the point where we no longer understand either orality or the nature of writing itself. As a matter of fact, written and oral sources are not mutually exclusive. They have common as well as autonomous characteristics, and specific functions which only either one can fill (or which one set of sources fills better than the other).

Therefore, they require different specific interpretative instruments. But the undervaluing and the overvaluing of oral sources end up by cancelling out specific qualities, turning these sources either into mere supports for traditional written sources, or into an illusory cure for all ills. This chapter will attempt to suggest some of the ways in which oral history is intrinsically different, and therefore specifically useful.

The orality of oral sources

Oral sources are *oral* sources. Scholars are willing to admit that the actual document is the recorded tape; but almost all go on to work on the transcripts, and it is only transcripts that are published.[2] Occasionally, tapes are actually destroyed: a symbolic case of the destruction of the spoken word.

The transcript turns aural objects into visual ones, which inevitably implies changes and interpretation. The different efficacy of recordings, as compared to transcripts—for classroom purposes, for instance—can only be appreciated by direct experience. This is one reason why I believe it is unnecessary to give excessive attention to the quest for new and closer methods of transcription. Expecting the transcript to replace the tape for scientific purposes is equivalent to doing art criticism on reproductions, or literary criticism on translations. The most literal translation is hardly ever the best, and a truly faithful translation always implies a certain amount of invention. The same may be true for transcription of oral sources.

The disregard of the orality of oral sources has a direct bearing on interpretative theory. The first aspect which is usually stressed is origin: oral sources give us information about illiterate people or social groups whose written history is either missing or distorted. Another aspect concerns content: the daily life and material culture of these people and groups. However, these are not specific to oral sources. Emigrants' letters, for instance, have the same origin and content, but are written. On the other hand, many oral history projects have collected interviews with members of social groups who use writing, and have been concerned with topics usually covered by the standard written archival material. Therefore, origin and content are not sufficient to distinguish oral sources from the range of sources used by social history in general; thus, many theories of oral history are, in fact, theories of social history as a whole.[3]

In the search for a distinguishing factor, we must therefore turn in the first place to form. We hardly need repeat here that writing represents language almost exclusively by means of segmentary traits (graphemes, syllables, words, and sentences). But language is also composed of another set of traits, which cannot be contained within a single segment but which are also bearers of meaning. The tone and volume range and the rhythm of popular speech carry implicit meaning and social connotations which are not reproducible in writing—unless, and then in inadequate and hardly accessible form, as musical notation.[4] The same statement may have quite contradictory meanings, according to the speaker's intonation, which cannot be represented objectively in the transcript, but only approximately described in the transcriber's own words.

In order to make the transcript readable, it is usually necessary to insert punctuation marks, which are always the more-or-less arbitrary addition of the transcriber. Punctuation indicates pauses distributed according to grammatical rules: each mark has a conventional place, meaning, and length. These hardly ever coincide with the rhythms and pauses of the speaking subject, and therefore end up by confining speech within grammatical and logical rules which it does not necessarily follow. The exact length and position of the pause has an important function in the understanding of the meaning of speech. Regular grammatical pauses tend to organize what is said around a basically expository and referential pattern, whereas pauses of irregular length and position accentuate the emotional content, and very heavy rhythmic pauses recall the style of epic narratives. Many narrators switch from one type of rhythm to another within the same interview, as their attitude toward the subjects under discussion changes. Of course, this can only be perceived by listening, not by reading.

A similar point can be made concerning the velocity of speech and its changes during the interview. There are no fixed interpretative rules: slowing down may mean greater emphasis as well as greater difficulty, and acceleration may show a wish to glide over certain points, as well as a greater familiarity or ease. In all cases, the analysis of changes in velocity must be combined with rhythm analysis. Changes are, however, the norm in speech, while regularity is the norm in writing (printing most of all) and the presumed norm of reading: variations are introduced by the reader, not by the text itself.

This is not a question of philological purity. Traits which cannot he contained within segments are the site (not exclusive, but very important) of essential narrative functions: they reveal the narrators' emotions, their participation in the story, and the way the story affected them. This often involves attitudes which speakers may not be able (or willing) to express otherwise, or elements which are not fully within their control. By abolishing these traits, we flatten the emotional content of speech down to the supposed equanimity and objectivity of the written document. This is even more true when folk informants are involved: they may be poor in vocabulary but are often richer in range of tone, volume and intonation than middle-class speakers who have learned to imitate in speech the monotone of writing.[5]

Oral history as narrative

Oral historical sources are *narrative* sources. Therefore the analysis of oral history materials must avail itself of some of the general categories developed by narrative theory in literature and folklore. This is as true of testimony given in free interviews as of the more formally organized materials of folklore.

For example, some narratives contain substantial shifts in the 'velocity' of narration, that is, in the ratio between the duration of the events described and the duration of the narration. An informant may recount in a few words experiences which lasted a long time, or dwell at length on brief episodes. These oscillations are significant, although we cannot establish a general norm of interpretation: dwelling on an episode may be a way of stressing its importance, but also a strategy to distract attentions from other more delicate points. In all cases, there is a relationship between the velocity of the narrative and the meaning of the narrator. The same can b said of other categories among those elaborated by Gerard Genette, such as 'distance' or 'perspective', which define the position of the narrator toward the story.[6]

Oral sources from nonhegemonic classes are linked to the tradition of the folk narrative. In this tradition distinctions between narrative genres are perceived differently than in the written tradition of the educated classes. This is true of the generic distinction between 'factual' and 'artistic' narratives, between 'events' and feeling or imagination. While the perception of an account as 'true' is relevant as much to legend as to personal experience and historical memory, there are no formal oral genres specifically destined to transmit historical information; historical, poetical, and legendary narratives often become inextricably mixed up.[7] The result is narratives in which the boundary between what takes place outside the narrator and what happens inside, between what concerns the individual and what concerns the group, may become more elusive than in established written genres, so that personal 'truth' may coincide with shared 'imagination'.

Each of these factors can be revealed by formal and stylistic factors. The greater or lesser presence of formalized materials (proverbs, songs, formulas, and stereotypes) may measure the degree in which a collective viewpoint exists within an individual's narrative. These shifts between standard language and dialect are often a sign of the kind of the control which speakers have over the narrative.

A typical recurring structure is that in which standard language is used overall, while dialect crops up in digressions or single anecdotes, coinciding with a more personal involvement of the narrator or (as when the occurrences of dialect coincide with formalized language) the intrusion of collective memory. On the other hand, standard language may emerge in a dialect narrative when it deals with themes more closely connected with the public sphere, such as politics. Again, this may mean both a more or less conscious degree of estrangement, or a process of 'conquest' of a more 'educated' form of expression beginning with participation in politics.[8] Conversely, the dialectization of technical terms may be a sign of the vitality of traditional speech and of the way in which speakers endeavor to broaden the expressive range of their culture.

Events and meaning

The first thing that makes oral history different, therefore, is that it tells us less about *events* than about their *meaning*. This does not imply that oral history has no factual validity. Interviews often reveal unknown events or unknown aspects of known events; they always cast new light on unexplored areas of the daily life of the nonhegemonic classes. From this point of view, the only problem posed by oral sources is that of verification (to which I will return in the next section).

But the unique and precious element which oral sources force upon the historian and which no other sources possess in equal measure is the speaker's subjectivity. If the approach to research is broad and articulated enough, a cross section of the subjectivity of a group or class may emerge. Oral sources tell us not just what people did, but what they wanted to do, what they believed they were doing, and what they now think they did. Oral sources may not add much to what we know, for instance, of the material cost of a strike to the workers involved, but they tell us a good deal about its psychological costs. Borrowing a literary category from the Russian formalists, we might say that oral sources, especially from nonhegemonic groups, are a very useful integration of other sources as far as the *fabula*—the logical, causal sequence of the story—goes; but they become unique and necessary because of their *plot*—the way in which the story materials are arranged by narrators in order to tell the story.[9]

The organization of the narrative reveals a great deal of the speakers' relationships to their history.

Subjectivity is as much the business of history as are the more visible 'facts'. What informants believe is indeed a historical *fact* (that is, the fact that they believe it), as much as what really happened. When workers in Terni misplace a crucial event of their history (the killing of Luigi Trastulli) from one date and context to another, this does not cast doubts on the actual chronology, but it does force us to arrange our interpretation of an entire phase of the town's history. When an old rank-and-file leader, also in Terni, dreams up a story about how he almost got the Communist Party to reverse its strategy after World War II, we do not revise our reconstructions of political debates within the Left, but learn the extent of the actual cost of certain decisions to those rank-and-file activists who had to bury into their subconscious their needs and desires for revolution. When we discover that similar stories are told in other parts of the country, we recognize the half-formed legendary complex in which the 'senile ramblings' of a disappointed old man reveal much about his party's history that is untold in the lengthy and lucid memoirs of its official leaders.[10]

Should we believe oral sources?

Oral sources are credible but with a *different* credibility. The importance of oral testimony may lie not in its adherence to fact, but rather in its departure from it, as imagination, symbolism, and desire emerge. Therefore, there are no 'false' oral sources. Once we have checked their factual credibility with all the established criteria of philological criticism and factual verification which are required by all types of sources anyway, the diversity of oral history consists in the fact that 'wrong' statements are still psychologically 'true' and that this truth may be equally as important as factually reliable accounts.

Of course, this does not mean that we accept the dominant prejudice which sees factual credibility as a monopoly of written documents. Very often, written documents are only the uncontrolled transmission of unidentified oral sources (as in the case of the report on Trastulli's death, which begins: 'According to verbal information taken . . .'). The passage from these oral '*ur*-sources' to the written document is often the result of processes which have no scientific credibility and are frequently heavy with class bias. In trial records (at least in Italy, where no legal value is accorded to the tape recorder or shorthand transcripts), what goes on record is not the words actually spoken by the witnesses, but a summary dictated by the judge to the clerk. The distortion inherent in such procedure is beyond assessment, especially when the speakers originally expressed themselves in dialect. Yet, many historians who turn up their noses at oral sources accept these legal transcripts with no questions asked. In a lesser measure (thanks to the frequent use of shorthand) this applies ***to*** parliamentary records, minutes of meetings and conventions, and interviews reported in newspapers: all sources which are legitimately and widely used in standard historical research.

A by-product of this prejudice is the insistence that oral sources are distant from events, and therefore undergo the distortion of faulty memory. Indeed, this problem exists for many written documents, which are usually written some time after the event to which they refer, and often by nonparticipants. Oral sources might compensate chronological distance with a much closer personal involvement. While written memoirs of politicians or labor leaders are usually credited until proven to be in error, they are as distant from some aspects of the event which they relate as are many oral history interviews, and only hide their dependence on time by assuming the immutable form of a 'text'. On the other hand, oral narrators have within their culture certain aids to memory. Many stories are told over and over, or discussed with members of the community; formalized narrative, even meter, may help preserve a textual version of an event.

In fact, one should not forget that oral informants may also be literate. Tiberio Ducci, a former leader of the farm workers' league in Genzano, in the Roman hills, may be atypical: in addition to remembering his own experience, he had also researched the local archives. But many informants read books and newspapers, listen to the radio and TV, hear sermons and political speeches, and keep diaries, letters, clippings, and photograph albums. Orality and writing, for many centuries now, have not existed separately: if many written sources are based on orality, modern orality itself is saturated with writing.

But what is really important is that memory is not a passive depository of facts, but an active proccss of creation of meanings. Thus, the specific utility of oral sources for the historian lies, not so much in their ability to preserve the past, as in the very changes wrought by memory. These changes reveal the narrators' effort to make sense of the past and to give a form to their lives, and set the interview and the narrative in their historical context.

Changes which may have subsequently taken place in the narrators' personal subjective consciousness or in their socioeconomic standing, may affect, if not the actual recounting of prior events, at least the valuation and the 'coloring' of the story. Several people are reticent, for instance, when it comes to describing illegal forms of struggle, such as sabotage. This does not mean that they do not remember them clearly, but that there has been a change in their political opinions, personal circumstances, or in their party's line. Acts considered legitimate and even normal or necessary in the past may be therefore now viewed as unacceptable and literally cast out of the tradition. In these cases, the most precious information may lie in what the informants *hide,* and in the fact that they *do* hide it, rather than in what they *tell.*

Often, however, narrators are capable of reconstructing their past attitudes even when they no longer coincide with present ones. This is the case with the Terni factory workers who admit that violent reprisals against the executives responsible for mass layoffs in 1953 may have been counterproductive, but yet reconstruct with great lucidity why they seemed useful and sensible at the time. In one of the most important oral testimonies of our time, *Autobiography of Malcolm X,* the narrator describes very vividly how his mind worked before he reached his present awareness, and then judges his own past self by the standards of his present political and religious consciousness. If the interview is conducted skillfully and its purposes are clear to the narrators, it is not impossible for them to make a distinction between present and past self, and to objectify the past self as other than the present one. In these cases—Malcolm X again is typical—*irony* is the major narrative mode: two different ethical (or political, or religious) and narrative standards interfere and overlap, and their tension shapes the telling of the story.

On the other hand, we may also come across narrators whose consciousness seems to have been arrested at climactic moments of their personal experience: certain Resistance fighters, or war veterans; and perhaps certain student militants of the 1960s. Often, these individuals are wholly absorbed by the totality of the historical event of which they were part, and their account assumes the cadences and wording of *epic*. The distinction between an ironic or an epic style implies a distinction between historical perspectives, which ought to be taken into consideration in our interpretation of the testimony.

Objectivity

Oral sources are not *objective*. This of course applies to every source, though the holiness of writing often leads us to forget it. But the inherent nonobjectivity of oral sources lies in specific intrinsic characteristics, the most important being that they are *artificial, variable, and partial*.

Alex Haley's introduction to *Autobiography of Malcolm X* describes how Malcolm shifted his narrative approach not spontaneously, but because the interviewer's questioning led him away from the exclusively public and official image of himself and of the Nation of Islam which he was trying to project. This illustrates the fact that the documents of oral history are always the result of a relationship, of a shared project in which both the interviewer and the interviewee are involved together, if not necessarily in harmony. Written documents are fixed; they exist whether we are aware of them or not, and do not change once we have found them. Oral testimony is only a potential resource until the researcher calls it into existence. The condition for the existence of the written source is emission; for oral sources, transmission: a difference similar to that described by Roman Jakobson and Piotr Bogatyrev between the creative processes of folklore and those of literature.[11]

The content of the written source is independent of the researcher's need and hypotheses; it is a stable text, which we can only interpret. The content of oral sources, on the other hand, depends largely on what the interviewer puts into it in terms of questions, dialogue, and personal relationship.

It is the researcher who decides that there will be an interview in the first place. Researchers often introduce specific distortions: informants tell them what they believe they want to be told and thus reveal who they think the researcher is. On the other hand, rigidly structured interviews may exclude elements whose existence or relevance were previously unknown to the interviewer and not contemplated in the question schedule. Such interviews tend to confirm the historian's previous frame of reference.

The first requirement, therefore, is that the researcher 'accept' the informant, and give priority to what she or he wishes to tell, rather than what the researcher wants to hear, saving any unanswered questions for later or for another interview. Communications always work both ways. The interviewees are always, though perhaps unobtrusively, studying the interviewers who 'study' them. Historians might as well recognize this fact and make the best of its advantages, rather than try to eliminate it for the sake of an impossible (and perhaps undesirable) neutrality.

The final result of the interview is the product of both the narrator and the researcher. When interviews, as is often the case, are arranged for publication omitting entirely the interviewer's voice, a subtle distortion takes place: the text gives the answers without the questions, giving the impression that a given narrator will always say the same things, no matter what the circumstances—in other words, the impression that a speaking person is as stable and repetitive as a written document. When the researcher's voice is cut out, the narrator's voice is distorted.

Oral testimony, in fact, is never the same twice. This is a characteristic of all oral communication, but is especially true of relatively unstructured forms, such as autobiographical or historical statements given in an interview. Even the same interviewer gets different versions from the same narrator at different times. As the two subjects come to know each other better, the narrator's 'vigilance' may be attenuated. Class subordination—trying to identify with what the narrator thinks is the interviewer's interest—may be replaced by more independence or by a better understanding of the purposes of the interview. Or a previous interview may have simply awakened memories which are then told in later meetings.

The fact that interviews with the same person may be continued indefinitely leads us to the question of the inherent incompleteness of oral sources. It is impossible to exhaust the entire memory of a single informant; the data extracted with each interview are always the result of a selection produced by the mutual relationship. Historical research with oral sources therefore always has the unfinished nature of a work in progress, In order to go through all the possible oral sources for the Terni strikes of 1949 to 1953, one ought to interview in depth several thousand people: any sample would only be as reliable as the sampling methods used, and could never guarantee against leaving out 'quality' narrators whose testimony alone might be worth ten statistically selected ones.

The unfinishedness of oral sources affects all other sources. Given that no research (concerning a historical time for which living memories are available) is complete unless it has exhausted oral as well as written sources, and that oral sources are inexhaustible, the ideal goal of going through 'all' possible sources becomes impossible. Historical work using oral sources is unfinished because of the nature of the sources; historical work excluding oral sources (where available) is incomplete by definition.

Who speaks in oral history?

Oral history is not where the working classes speak for themselves. The contrary statement, of course, would not be entirely unfounded: the recounting of a strike through the words and memories of workers rather than those of the police and the (often unfriendly) press obviously helps (though not automatically) to balance a distortion implicit in those sources. Oral sources are a necessary (not a sufficient) condition for a history of the nonhegemonic classes; they are less necessary (though by no means useless) for the history of the ruling classes, who have had control over writing and leave behind a much more abundant written record.

Nevertheless, the control of historical discourse remains firmly in the hands of the historian. It is the historian who selects the people who will be interviewed; who contributes to the shaping of the testimony by asking the questions and reacting to the answers; and who gives the testimony its final published shape and context (if only in terms of montage and transcription). Even accepting that the working class speaks through oral history, it is clear that the class does not speak in the abstract, but speaks *to* the historian, *with* the historian and, inasmuch as the material is published, *through* the historian.

Indeed, things may also be the other way around. The historian may validate his or her discourse by 'ventriloquizing' it through the narrator's testimony. So far from disappearing in the objectivity of the sources, the historian remains important at least as a partner in dialogue, often as a 'stage director' of the interview, or as an 'organizer' of the testimony. Instead of discovering sources, oral historians partly create them. Far from becoming mere mouthpieces for the working class, oral historians may be using other people's words, but are still responsible for the overall discourse.

Much more than written documents, which frequently carry the impersonal aura of the institutions by which they are issued even though, of course, they are composed by individuals, of whom we often know little or nothing—oral sources involve the entire account in their own subjectivity. Alongside the first person narrative of the interviewee stands the first person of the historian, without whom there would be no interview. Both the informant's and the historian's discourse are in narrative form, which is much less frequently the case with archival documents. Informants are historians, after a fashion; and the historian is, in certain ways, a part of the source.

Traditional writers of history present themselves usually in the role of what literary theory would describe as an 'omniscient narrator'. They give a third-person account of events of which they were not a part, and which they dominate entirely and from above (above the consciousness of the participants themselves). They appear to be impartial and detached, never entering the narrative except to give comments aside, after the manner of some nineteenth-century novelists. Oral history changes the writing of history much as the modern novel transformed the writing of literary fiction: the most important change is that the narrator is now pulled into the narrative and becomes a party of the story.

This is not just a grammatical shift from the third to the first person, but a whole new narrative attitude. The narrator is now one of the characters, and the *telling* of the story is part of the story being told. This implicitly indicates a much deeper political and personal involvement than that of the external narrator. Writing radical oral history, then, is not a matter of ideology, of subjective sides-taking, or of choosing one set of sources instead of another. It is, rather, inherent in the historian's presence in the story, in the assumption of responsibility—which inscribes her or him in the account and reveals historiography as an autonomous act of narration. Political choices become less visible and vocal, but more basic.

The myth that the historian as a subject might disappear in the objective truth of working-class sources was part of a view of political militancy as the annihilation of all subjective roles into that of the full-time activist, and as absorption into an abstract working class. This resulted in an ironical similarity to the traditional attitude which saw historians as not subjectvely involved in the history which they were writing. Oral historians appear to yield to other subjects of discourse, but, in fact, the historian becomes less and less of a 'go-between' from the working class to the reader, and more and more of a protagonist.

In the writing of history, as in literature, the act of focusing on the function of the narrator causes this function to be fragmented. In a novel such as Joseph Conrad's *Lord Jim,* the character/narrator Marlow can recount only what he himself has seen and heard; in order to tell the 'whole story', he is forced to take several other 'informants' into his tale. The same thing happens to historians working with oral sources. On explicitly entering the story, historians must allow the sources to enter the tale with their autonomous discourse.

Oral history has no unified subject; it is told from a multitude of points of view, and the impartiality traditionally claimed by historians is replaced by the partiality of the narrator. 'Partiality' here stands for both 'unfinishedness' and for 'taking sides': oral history can never be told without taking sides, since the 'sides' exist inside the telling. And, no matter what their personal histories and beliefs may be, historians and 'sources' are hardly ever on the same 'side'. The confrontation of their different partialities—confrontation as 'conflict', and confrontation as 'search for unity'—is one of the things which make oral history interesting.

Notes

1. B. Placido in *L Repubblica,* 3 October 1978.
2. One Italian exception is the Istituto Ernesto De Martino, an independent radical research organization based in Milan, which has published 'sound archives' on long-playing records since the mid-l960s—without anyone in the cultural establishment noticing: see F. Coggiola, 'L'attività dell'Istituto Ernesto de Martino', in D. Carpitella (ed.), *L'etnomusicologia in Italia,* Palermo: Flaccovio, 1975, pp. 265–270.
3. L. Passerini, 'Sull'utilità e il danno delle fonti orali pcr la storia'. Introduction to Passerini (ed.), *Storia Orale. Vito quotidiana e cultura materiale delle classi subalterne,* Torino: Rosenberg & Sellier, 1978, discusses the relationship of oral history and social history.

4. On musical notation as reproduction of speech sounds, see G. Marini, 'Musica popolare e parlato popolare urbano', in Circolo Gianni Bosio (ed.), *I giorni contati*, Milano: Mazzotta, 1958, pp. 33–34. A. Lomax, *Folk Song Styles and Culture,* Washington DC: American Association for the Advancement of Sciences, 1968, Publication no. 88, discusses electronic representation of vocal styles.
5. See W. Labov, 'The logic of non-standard English', in L. Kampf and P. Lauter (eds), *The Politics of Literature,* New York: Random House, 1970, pp. 194–244, on the expressive qualities of non-standard speech.
6. In this article, I use these terms as defined and used by G. Genette, *Figures Ill,* Paris: Seuil, 1972.
7. On genre distinctions in folk and oral narrative, see D. Ben-Amos, 'Categories analytiques et genres populaires', *Poétique,* 1974, no. 19, pp. 268–293; and J. Vansina, *Oral Tradition,* Harmondsworth: Penguin Books, [1961], 1973.
8. For instance, G. Bordoni, Communist activist from Rome, talked about family and community mainly in dialect, but shifted briefly to a more standardized form of Italian whenever he wanted to reaffirm his allegiance to the party. The shift showed that, although he accepted the party's decisions, they remained other than his direct experience. His recurring idiom was 'There's nothing you can do about it.' See Circolo Gianni Bosio, *I giorni cantati,* pp. 58–66.
9. On fabula and plot see B. Tomaševskji, 'Sjužetnoe postroenie', in *Teorija literatury Poetika,* Moscow Leningrad, 1928; Italian trans., 'La costruzione dell'intreccio', in T. Todorov (ed.), *I formalisti russi,* Torino: Einaudi, 1968, published as *Théorie de la littérature,* Paris: Seuil, 1965.
10. These stories are discussed in chapters 1 and 6 of A. Portelli, *The Death of Luigi Trastulli,* Albany: State University of New York Press, 1991.
11. R. Jakobson and P. Bogatyrev, 'Le folklore forme spécifique de creation', in R. Jakobson, *Questions de poétique,* Paris: Seuil, 1973, pp. 59–72.

A Dialogical Relationship: An Approach to Oral History

1. Oral sources and oral history

The phrase *oral history* is a common abbreviation for what we might describe, more articulately, as *the use of oral sources in history or the social sciences.*[1] In its most elementary form, the *oral narratives and testimony* which constitute oral history are but an additional tool in the historian's panoply of sources, and are therefore subject to the same critical scrutiny as all other sources, in order to ascertain their reliability and their usefulness. From this point of view, we distinguish the oral *source* from the oral *tradition*: the latter is made up of verbal constructs that are formalized, transmitted, shared, whereas the historian's oral sources are individual, informal, dialogic narratives created in the encounter between the historian and the narrator. Of course, these narratives may incorporate traditional materials, and oral historians may also avail themselves of oral traditions. However, it is best to keep the two concepts distinct: not all that is oral is traditional.

However, when we speak of *oral history* we also mean something more specific. Rather than an additional, often secondary tool in the historian's panoply, oral sources are used as the axis of another type of historical work, in which questions of memory, narrative, subjectivity, dialogue shape the historian's very agenda. When this is the case, the critical use of oral sources requires specific approaches and procedures, adequate to their specific nature and form.

As opposed to the majority of historical documents, in fact, oral sources are not *found*, but *co-created* by the historian. They would not exist in this form without the presence, and stimulation, the active role of the historian in the field interview. Oral sources are generated in a dialogic exchange—an *interview*—literally a looking at each other, an exchange of gazes. In this exchange questions and answers do not necessarily go in one direction only. The historian's agenda must meet the agenda of the narrator; what the historian wishes to know may not necessarily coincide with what the narrator wishes to tell.

As a consequence, the whole agenda of the research may be radically revised. For instance, when I started a project on the history of the labor movement from 1949 to 1953 in Terni, an industrial town in Central Italy, many narrators insisted in connecting the events I was interested in to the long-term history of their families and their town. Though this was not what I was originally looking for, I revised my project, and gained a great deal by it. Eventually, I ended up writing a history of the town from 1831 to 1985.[2]

Oral history, then, is primarily a *listening art.* Even when the dialogue stays within the original agenda, historians may not always be aware that certain questions need to be asked. Often, indeed, the most important information lies outside what both the historian and the narrator think of as historically relevant. For instance: I recently carried out a project on the memory of Nazi massacre perpetrated in Rome in 1944, known as the massacre of the Fosse Ardeatine. 335 men were executed in retaliation for a partisan action that killed a number of German soldiers in the center of Rome. Beyond the reconstruction of the events, I wanted to understand how the survivors, especially women, had lived with the loss and the memory, how they had made lives for themselves with this pain in their souls afterwards. It was only by accident, however, and when I thought that the interview was over, that I stumbled into one of the most painful memories.

I had been interviewing Ms. Ada Pignotti, who was 23 when her husband and three other relatives were killed by the Nazis at the Fosse Ardeatine. She had told me about those days, and then about her life ever since. We both thought the interview was over, that all that needed to be said had been said and I had no more questions. However, we chatted on—and I left the tape running—as she told me about her protracted, humiliating struggle with bureaucracy in order to receive the small pension to which she was entitled as a victim.

Then, almost incidentally, she said: 'And wherever you'd go, they knew that I had lost my husband, I and the others, the other women—and they all tried, wanted, tried to give you a line, a talk all of their own, because—who knows: you had to be at their disposal. You were a woman, you had no husband anymore, so you could very well …'[3] Pain, loss, poverty—these were themes to be expected. What I did not expect was this insult, almost unspeakable (as the narrator's reticence shows), an insult for which she didn't even have a word—sexual harassment—at the time.

Fortunately, I had left the tape running. Though I thought the interview was over, I knew that the art of listening includes respect; and you don't show respect by turning the tape recorder off, as if to announce to your interviewee that from now on you are no longer interested in what she may have to say. Thus, the unexpected theme of harassment came into my research, and later on I was able to find confirmation in other interviews. No one had talked about it before; even the widows had hardly discussed it among themselves. It was too private to mention in public and, most importantly, until recently neither historians nor the women themselves were aware that this, too, was history. The assumption was that the historical event was the massacre; the survivors were supposed to be interesting only as witnesses to it, but their own lives were irrelevant. And, of course, women's history and the history of sexuality were not considered of historical significance when these elderly ladies studied history in school.

Oral history, however, is not only about the event. It is about the place and meaning of the event within the lives of the tellers; which is why, in order to understand the meaning of two days in 1944, I had to go back and forward two or three generations, from 1870 to 1999.

2. Relationship: dialogue

All of this means that oral history is a listening art, and an art based on a set of relationships:

- the relationship between interviewees and interviewers (dialogue);
- the relationship between the time in which the dialogue takes place, and the historical time discussed in the interview (memory);
- the relationship between the public and the private sphere, between autobiography and history—between, we might say, History and story;
- the relationship between the orality of the source and the writing of the historian.

Let us begin with the first of these relationships—dialogue. A young scholar who was interviewing women who had breast cancer surgery once told me this story. She was talking to an elderly, recently widowed lady, who had spoken at length about many things but had carefully avoided the theme of the interview. The lady's desire to protect her intimacy crossed the researcher's desire to know about her experience, so she wouldn't talk about it. Yet, her own need for human contact, so all-important for a person who has been left alone, made her want to continue to conversation, so she talked of other things. Only incidentally (and this time with the tape recorder off) the young researcher mentioned that she, too, had had surgery for breast cancer. Right there, the relationship changed: 'so you're one of us', the lady said. Authority, always implicit in an interview situation, also shifted: rather than feeling that she was under the researcher's scrutinizing gaze, the lady felt that her age placed her now in a position of authority—'but you're only a child!', she said. It was then that the definition of interview as mutual exchange of gazes was radically revised and literalized, as the two women bared their breasts and compared their scars.[4]

'You are one of us/you are only a child'—the interview is based on a common ground that makes dialogue possible, but also on a difference that makes it meaningful. It would be a mistake to assume that only similarity allows interviewees to express themselves, that only similarity establishes the 'trust' on which dialogue is founded. By definition, in fact, an exchange of knowledge has a meaning only if this knowledge is not previously shared—if, that is, between the subjects involved there exists a meaningful difference and one of them is in a learning situation.

For instance, in a project I coordinated in 1990, a group of my students and I were collecting interviews on the historical memory of the students in my department, in order to explore the cultural and political roots of a nation-wide student movement. We soon realized that the fact that both the interviewers and the interviewees were students, and involved in the movement, ultimately paralyzed the dialogue: 'Why are you asking me about this? You're supposed to know it already!' Also, the fact that their own peers took upon themselves a role of authority as interviewers seemed to some students an undue assertion of authority. On the other hand, when the interviews were done by me, the hierarchical difference between me as a professor and them as students was less a problem for the interviewees than an opportunity to explain certain things to someone, a professor, who didn't know them ('You professors don't know a thing about what's on the students' minds!'). Thus, my difference, and the fact that I was in a position of learning from them reversed our usual authority roles and made the conversation meaningful.[5]

Perhaps the most important lesson I received in field work was when a black, working-class, American woman told me—a white, middle-class, European male—'I don't trust you'—and then went on for two hours, telling stories that implicitly explained why she didn't.[6] Common ground makes communication possible, but difference makes it meaningful. Common ground does not have to mean a shared identity but must rather depend on a shared will to listen to and accept each other critically. In this case, the possibility of dialogue was established initially both by the fact that I had been introduced by trusted friends from the Highlander Center. It was confirmed by the first question asked in the conversation—not by me, but by the lady's husband, a preacher, union organizer, and former coal miner. As I have already pointed out, questions are not a one-way thing. He opened the conversation by asking me a question: 'Are you in the United Mine Workers?' When I explained that I was not in the UMWA, but was a member of the teachers' union back home, then the interview could begin. Finally, what enabled the interview to go on was the fact that I asked no probing, indiscreet questions. I mostly listened to what they had to say. They could see that I was not studying them, but learning from them.

Another example. The same people from Highlander who had introduced me to this black couple who later suggested I also interview Annie Napier, a disabled miner's wife in Harlan, Kentucky. I called her, and she told me to come over. Then—as she revealed several years later—she called her sister and asked her, 'What shall we do?' They finally reached the following conclusion: 'If he ain't too stuck up, we'll talk to him.' It was only years later that I thought of asking her, 'How did you know I wasn't too stuck up?' And she said: 'You came into the house and didn't look for a clean place to set your butt on.' Which also suggests another thing: there is no one-way relationship between the observer and the observed. The observed also observes us, and judges us from behaviors of which we are not even aware (like the farmer in Tuscany who deduced my political leanings from the fact that, as he explained to a friend, 'He didn't ask me about priests.' Sometimes, it's the questions we *don't* ask that open up the dialogue).

In other words: it is the historian's openness to listening and to dialogue, and the respect for the narrators, that establishes a mutual acceptance based on difference and thus opens up the narrative space for the interviewee to go into. On the other hand, it is the interviewee's willingness to talk and open up to some degree that enables the historians to do their work. And the historians' openness about themselves and the purpose of their work is a crucial factor in creating this space.

3. Relationships: The public and the private

Let us go on to another form of relationship, that between the public and the private sphere. One reason why the story of sexual harassment to the widows of the Fosse Ardeatine massacre had never been told before was that it was thought of as a personal matter, of no historical interest. Indeed, we would have looked in vain for its traces in public archives or court records.

Oral sources, then, help us question the boundary between what is of concern to history and what it not. On the one hand, both parties are caught in a grid of pre-established categories of relevance. Historians often do not know that there are unforeseen areas of experience that they ought to explore; narrators may not always be aware of the historical relevance of their personal experience. They may wish to guard them as too intimate to be revealed, or may be reluctant to discuss things that are important to them lest they be dismissed by the historian as irrelevant. This is why 'I have nothing to say' or 'What do you want me to say?' are such common beginnings in interviews. Even persons who have much to say, and may be anxious to say it, may be worried that their precious narrative may not be recognized, may not be 'History' as they have been taught to define it.

In fact, the shifting and elusive boundary between History and stories is one of the relationships that make oral history meaningful. Ultimately, oral history is about the historical significance of personal experience on the one hand, and the personal impact of historical matters on the other. The hard core of oral history lies exactly at this point, where history breaks into private lives (for instance: when war breaks into domestic space in the shape of a bomb dropped from an airplane) or when private lives are drawn into history (for instance: the experience of the trenches in World War I, the experience of Italian troops in Russian campaign in World War II...).

Yet, after listening to so many war narratives by men, I wondered: is there a comparable women's narrative about personal encounters with the public sphere? When I was working on the project on Terni, I did my own transcribing, which was hard and gruelling work. Thus, I used to skip certain sections of the interviews which I thought I would not use in the book. After a while, I realized that the narratives I skipped fell mainly into two categories: men's war stories, and women's hospital tales, most specifically tales about assisting relatives in hospitals. War stories seemed too common, and not 'local' enough; hospital tales seemed private, not 'political' and not local. But the fact that these were the stories I was ignoring drew my attention to their analogies. I realized that the confrontation with death and suffering that took place in war for men also took place in hospitals for women; also, both the war stories and the hospital narratives were about the experience in which respectively men and women leave home to enter the public sphere and confront the State, authority, bureaucracy, technology, science. Just as men told stories about confronting the brass and proving that they knew more than the officers, likewise women relished narratives in which they put those big doctors in their place and corrected their errors. In other words, women's hospital narratives were the equivalent of men's war tales: stories about the encounter of private persons with the public sphere (it all comes together, of course, in the stories of war nurses, as in Vietnam).

The difference, of course, lies in the fact that, while the historical significance of the war experience is generally recognized, the women's hospital narrative has been generally neglected by historians and confined to a merely private and familiar sphere. By insisting on telling these stories, the women narrators forced me to stop and listen and to recognize how important they were. In other words, oral history allows us to access the historicity of private lives—but, most importantly, it forces to redefine our pre-conceived notion of the geography of public and private space and their relationship.

4. Relationships: Memory

From the point of view of traditional, more methodologically conservative historians, the most important objection to oral sources concerned their reliability: one cannot rely on oral narratives because memory and subjectivity tend to 'distort' the facts.

In the first place, this is not always the case—also, how can we be sure that equally serious distortions are not to be found also in more established documentary sources? Thus, as with all other sources, the task of the historian lies in cross-checking the information, checking each narrative against other narratives and other kinds of sources.

In the second place, and most importantly, the most critically advanced and methodologically aware work in oral history has turned the question upon its head: what makes oral sources important and fascinating is precisely the fact that they do not passively record the facts, but elaborate upon them and create meaning through the labor of memory and the filter of language. Which is why I, personally, tend to avoid the use of terms such as 'testimony' and 'witness', and prefer to speak of 'narratives' and 'narrators', 'stories' and 'story-tellers' or, in fact, 'history tellers'.[7]

When we work with oral sources, then, we must chart a complex path covering three distinct but interconnected levels: a fact of the past, the historical event; a fact of the present, the narrative we hear; and a long-lasting, fluid relationship, the interplay between these two facts. Thus, the work of the oral historian includes:

- historiography in its traditional meaning (reconstructing past events);
- anthropology, cultural analysis, textual criticism (interpreting the interview);
- and the space in between (how do those events produce this memory and this narrative).

Oral history, then, is history of events, history of memory, and history and interpretation of events through memory. Memory, in fact, is not a mere depository of information, but rather an ongoing process of elaboration and re\construction of meaning. At this time, when the very meaning of Italian democracy undergoes a drastic right-wing revision based on debunking the foundational narrative of anti-Fascist Resistance, the history of memory is at least as important and as necessary as the history of the events.

Indeed, events are recognized as such, and become sites of meaning, primarily through the work of personal and public memory, which select certain events out of the shapeless array of everyday happenings, and endow them with meaning. Interrogating the wrong memory, especially when it is so widely shared, is a way of interrogating the meaning of the remembered event. In order to do this interpretive work on false narratives, we must be able to prove that they are indeed false. Thus, the oral historian's work includes a careful check of the facts to the best of our abilities, so that we may distinguish between factually reliable narratives, which are the majority, and the significant cases of creative error and myth. Only after we have done this work, by cross-checking false memories with the reconstruction of the events, we are able to gauge their impact—as in the case of the Fosse Ardeatine massacre and its background—in social imagination and in the contemporary political arena. At this point, even error, invention, misunderstanding, even lies, especially when they are socially widespread, become precious symptoms of such important historical processes as memory and desire.

5. Narrative responsibility

Just like memory, the narrative itself is not a fixed text and depository of information, but rather a process and a performance. As Walter J. Ong writes, orality does not generate texts[8], but *performances*: in orality, we are not dealing with finished discourse but with discourse in the making (indeed, *dialogic* discourse in the making). Thus, when we talk of oral history we ought to think in terms of verbs rather than nouns—*remembering* rather than *memory*; *telling* rather than *tale*. In this way, we can think of oral sources as something happening in the present, rather than just as a testimony of the past.

Most importantly, when we look at the act of speech, rather than at its outcome, we realize that remembering and telling are indeed influenced by the historical context and by the social frameworks of memory[9], but they are also filtered by individual responsibility. The place where memory is elaborated is the individual's mind, and the way we access it is the individual narrative. Therefore, narrators take a responsibility upon themselves, each time they tell their history. We must always remember this: just as the narrator has a responsibility to tell, the historian has a responsibility to open up a narrative space by listening actively to what the narrator has to tell.

6. Relationships: Orality and writing

The form of the oral history document is one of performance and dialogue; the form of the historian's work is that of a written, monologic essay. When we present the results of an oral history project, then, we must take care to leave at least a trace of the oral, narrative, dialogic origin of the materials we work with. This is why, beyond a matter of documentary accuracy, oral historians quote their sources and use montage to a much wider extent than other historians, anthropologists, sociologists.

By quoting our narrators at length, we also achieve another result: that of retaining at least some of the complex polysemy of oral story-telling. On the one hand, by preserving, as much as it is possible in writing, the vernacular, colloquial language in which the stories are often told, we insist that the meaning of an event cannot be separated from the language in which it is remembered and narrated. On the other hand, the narrative form always contains more layers of meaning, more directions of interpretation than a logical, rational analysis. Although we do not refrain from advancing hypotheses and suggesting interpretations, we are aware of the fact that the material we present can always be read in a number of different ways. Indeed, it has often been the case that other readers, or the narrators themselves, saw in my own books undercurrents of meaning and webs of connections which I had not intentionally put there, and of which I had not been aware myself.

Orality, then, is not just the vehicle of information but also a component of its meaning. The dialogic and narrative form of oral sources culminate in the density and complexity of language itself. The very tones and accents of the oral discourse convey the history and identity of the speakers, and transmit meanings well beyond the speakers' conscious intention.

7. Conclusions

Now, the important thing about the dialogic nature of oral history work is that it does not end with the interview, or even with the publication, but must find ways of being useful to the individuals and the communities involved. This is the process that goes under the generic labels of 'restitution' and 'dissemination'.

Restitution, of course, begins with the interview itself—in the first place, at least returning a copy of the tape to the interviewee, or to the family. In the past, this was not always easy. On the one hand, duplicating was not an easy process before the availability of electronic tools. Most importantly, often our interviewees, especially in rural environments, did not own a tape or cassette recorder and were unable to listen to the tapes. They, however, accepted them gladly, both as a token of our good will, and as something to pass on to the younger generations. More recently, especially since we have been able to put the catalogue of our archive on the web, we have received requests from family members, especially grandchildren, of our interviewees of the '60s and '70s, and were glad to be able to return copies of the recordings to them. In this way, we help create stores for family memories.

Things become more complicated when it comes to restitution to the community, because it involves locating an institution, an organization, that can be identified as active in and representative of, the community. While we have done our best to locate copies of the tapes in local libraries and archives, this was not always the best solution, as the collections remained largely unused.

We had better luck with schools, not so much in terms of depositing the material, as of teaching classes on our research on the community's history and culture. This work often resulted in an increased awareness of cultural identity and of projects that the young people could carry out themselves. An even more effective form of restitution was in terms of music, theatre, media. I remember a wonderful evening in which we went back to Arrone, a town where I had collected many songs of anti-fascism and union struggle, and presented a program based on those very songs. The very fact that a group of professional musicians from Rome had found those songs important enough to learn and sing them was a revelation to the community that had been taking them for granted. More recently, the Circolo Bosio has produced a series of multimedia documents (DVD, CD-Rom) that have been distributed to schools and libraries in local communities (Terni, Tivoli, Valmontone, Monterotondo) and have become important teaching tools. An interesting case was the CD-ROM we produced in 2003, to commemorate the 50 years since the mass layoffs at the Terni steel works: as it came out exactly at the time of another wave of mass layoffs, we gave out dozens of copies to the workers on the picket lines at the factory, and it became an instant organizing tool.

Another thing we should keep in mind is that by 'community' we may not necessarily mean a geographic community, but also a community of feeling and action. This is the case of the 'alternative globalization' movement that staged the mass protests at Genoa in 2001 (culminating with the death of a young demonstrator). We have carried out an oral history project on those events, and produced a number of home-made audio CDs that were both distributed among the movement, and sold to finance the cost of legal defence in a number of court cases that followed the protest. In this case, we may also notice that, since the project was carried out mainly by young researchers who were themselves part of the movement, it is the 'community' itself that produces the research and its results.

Another case is my research on the massacre of the Fosse Ardeatine. The episode had been cloaked in a cloud of false narratives and legends that were offensive both to the Resistance, and to the victims themselves. The most important aspect of 'restitution' was the kind of historical rectification and recognition that the book granted to the 'communities' of the partisans and to the survivors. Because the book was (relatively) successful, they felt that they had been vindicated, and that their voices had been articulated so that they could no longer be ignored. The book was published in 1999; since then, I have been involved in at least 150 events with partisans and survivors, in schools, meetings, festivals, telling the story along with them. The book has also been used as a teaching tool in many schools.

This experience suggests that 'restitution' is a somewhat inadequate label. The historian/activist contribution to those 'communities' is, in fact, not just the collection of the stories and songs. Nor is it just to return the knowledge to the community (which, by definition, already possess it, since that's where it comes from in the first place). Rather, the historian/activist's contribution to the community is an elaboration and articulation of the community's knowledge, and the spreading of this knowledge beyond the community's boundaries.

Thus, the most important contribution I feel I have made to the communities has been, often, the fact that my work made their knowledge available to artists that told their story all over the country. Ascanio Celestini has presented a one-man performance on the Fosse Ardeatine in hundreds of venues all over Italy; singer Giovanna Marini (Italy's finest musician) wrote, performed and recorded a ballad based on the narratives in my book. In other words, the non-academic uses of the book not only returned the pride and identity to the partisans and survivors, but restored an awareness of these events and their meaning to a broad national community.

This, of course, is only one—though possibly the most significant—example of a non-academic use of oral history. After all, the cultural/activist tradition with which I identify myself—that of the Istituto de Martino, the Circolo Gianni Bosio, the Nuovo Canzoniere Italiano—has been active entirely outside the academy (my own academic position has nothing to do with oral history and folk music). Our purpose has been, from the beginning, to document the musical and historical knowledge of the urban and rural working classes in order to develop forms of communication—concerts, recordings, teach-ins, theatre, radio programs as well as books and articles—that would reinforce working people's sense of identity and cohesion and articulate their ideals and grievances.

The synthesis of this approach is that we need to combine the best of activist involvement with people and communities, with the best of the 'academic' methodology, so that the dialogic result of the work we produce jointly will not be a mere mirroring of what the community already knows, but a further articulation of this knowledge, and its inclusion in a broader cultural dialogue. After all, what makes Terni steel workers proud and aware of their heritage is less the fact that I returned the tapes of their interviews. Instead, because my book based on their stories is a textbook in a number of universities in the United States and elsewhere, their experience and their words are now part of an international historical record from which they had been excluded before.

Finally, a dialogue reflects on both sides. An interview is primarily a learning situation for the interviewer, especially if the motivation is (broadly) political. It is hard for me to pinpoint ways in which doing oral history and collecting folk songs has changed me: I have been doing this for thirty-five years, and I guess I can say that most of who and what I am is a result of this work. Perhaps, the most important thing I have learned is the art of listening and respecting the agendas and priorities of other people. I hope I have been able to apply this lesson, to some extent at least, not only in oral history work but also in my own life.

Notes

1. Gianni Bosio, 'Fonti orali e storiografia,' in *L'intellettuale rovesciato* (Milan: Edizioni Bella Ciao, 1975), pp. 263–68.
2. Alessandro Portelli, *Biografia di una città. Storia e racconto: Terni 1831–1985* (Torino: Einaudi, 1985). For more introductory readings on oral history, see Paul Thompson, *The Voice of the Past: Oral History* (Oxford University Press, 1988); *The Oral History Reader*, ed. Robert Perks and Alistair Thomson (London: Routledge, 1998); *Oral History. An Interdisciplinary Anthology*, second edition, Altamira Press (London,

1996), ed. David Dunawaye Willa K. Baum; the journal *Historia, Antropología y Fuente Oral*, published in Barcelona, Spain.

3. In Alessandro Portelli, *The Order Has Been Carried Out* (New York: Palgrave, 2003), p. 219.
4. The research was never published; for reasons of privacy, I cannot supply the names of the persons involved.
5. Micaela Arcidiacono et al., *L'aeroplano e le stelle. Storia orale di una realtà studentesca* (Rome: Manifestolibri, 1994).
6. A. Portelli, 'There's Always Goin' Be a Line: History-Telling as a Multivocal Art', in *The Battle of Valle Giulia. Oral History and the Art of Dialogue* (Madison: Wisconsin University Press, 1997), pp. 24–39.
7. See Alessandro Portelli, 'Oral History as Genre' and 'There's Always Goin' Be a Line: History-Telling as a Multivocal Art', in *The Battle of Valle Giulia. Oral History and the Art of Dialogue* (Madison: Wisconsin University Press, 1997), pp. 3–39.
8. Walter J. Ong, *Orality and Literacy. The Technologizing of the Word* (London and New York: Methuen, 1982), pp. 10–15.
9. Maurice Halbwachs, *La mémoire collective* (Paris: Presses Universitaires de France, 1968).